CARE OF THE DYING
A CATHOLIC PERSPECTIVE

The Catholic Health Association
of the United States
St. Louis

Cover illustration by Scott Hunt.

Second Printing – June 1993

The Catholic Health Association of the United States
4455 Woodson Road
St. Louis, MO 63134-3797

ISBN 0-87125-213-9

Printed in the United States of America.
Printed on recycled paper.

CONTENTS

PART IV

PREFACE

Death will always be seen as an intrusion, coming too soon, too early, before a life has been completed. By the end of the twentieth century we have devised, through human dedication and ingenuity, the means to defer the time and to control the manner of dying. We have attained unprecedented success in the diagnosis and treatment of illness, in the use of technology for prolonging and in some cases even restoring life, in the application of pharmacological and other resources for controlling extreme pain, and in psychotherapeutic approaches to easing anxiety, anger — all the emotions that may accompany the profound separation that is death. Yet is it not one of the paradoxes of our times that we appear increasingly preoccupied, terrified, even denying of death? The widespread anticipation of dying as a "tortuous" process characterized by extraordinary pain, solitude, and expense is reflected in the increasing public and professional support for physician assisted suicide as a humane alternative to an institutional and technologically managed death.

Christian faith, with its valuing of human life here and now and its belief in eternal life in God, says that a new approach to dying is possible. This faith, rooted in the gospel of Jesus Christ, teaches us to love our earthly life and to love our eternal life, for love of life is indivisible. Our faith in God and love of life create an unshakable assurance about illness, dying, and death. Therefore,

- We need not cling fearfully to life as the last thing we possess, but can commit ourselves in freedom, detachment, and confidence to an absolutely last, absolutely first reality that is God.
- While a struggle for health can be meaningful, a struggle against death at all costs — an effort that becomes a torment — is nonsense.
- The physician, the nurse, and other caregivers will not see death as an enemy or as personal defeat; rather they are able to accompany the dying person to the end.
- The dying person will be integrated within the circle of family and of professional caregivers where the task is not restricted to providing medical treatment but consists in the human devotion of all.

To clarify and to extend this insight of Catholic theological teaching is one of the priorities of the Catholic Health Association of the United States. To this end, it convened in October 1990 a group of its membership, representing the various professional disciplines that must address the issues in caring for persons at the end of life. The experience and wisdom of this group found expression first in the design of a document that would describe the cultural, social-political, clinical contexts, as well as the theological, moral, and pastoral response. After a series of CHA staff editions with suggestions from members of the 1990 work group, the document reached its final form through a creative rewriting and editing by Rev. Richard Gula, SS, with assistance from Rev. Robert Kinast.

The effort to bring the Catholic perspective on care of the dying to all of CHA members reaches beyond this foundational document, *Care of the Dying: A Catholic Perspective*, into two further resources. The first is a set of four comprehensive educational modules designed for leaders who are the key to integrating the Catholic theological, moral, and pastoral perspective in care of the dying: trustees and sponsors, administrative leaders, clinical leaders, and mission leaders. The second is a set of resources to assist those who often become spokespersons in the public sector in understanding and articulating a deeper message about living and dying: the media and legislative advocates.

We are grateful to all who have contributed to these works. Their experience, insight, and generosity have been at the same time inspirational and invaluable in enabling us to achieve the goals of this two-year project. We hope that our readers will find something of the richness of the experience in using them that we enjoyed in producing them.

ACKNOWLEDGMENTS

The Catholic Health Association of the United States expresses gratitude to the following members of task forces convened to advise CHA on various issues in its End of Life project:

The Catholic Tradition Speaks to Suffering and Dying

Ronald G. Blankenbaker, MD
St. Vincent Hospital & Health Care Center
Indianapolis, IN

Robert Castagna
Oregon Catholic Conference
Portland, OR

Barbara Cox
Dominican Health Services
Spokane, WA

Sr. Rhea Emmer, CSA
Sisters of Agnes Convent
Foun du Lac, WI

Thomas E. Hooyman, PhD
St. John's Mercy Medical Center
St. Louis, MO

Steven H. Miles, MD
Hennepin County Medical Center
Minneapolis, MN

Neil Parent, PhD
United States Catholic Conference
Washington, DC

Katherine Butler
Greensfelder, Hemker & Gale, PC
St. Louis, MO

Matthew Connolly, MD
University of California
Los Angeles, CA

Doris Donnelly, PhD
John Carroll University
University Heights, OH

Rev. Richard Gula, SS, PhD
St. Patrick's Seminary
Menlo Park, CA

Rev. Charles Hudson
Center for Hope Hospice
Roselle, NJ

Rev. Gerald Niklas
Good Samaritan Hospital
Cincinnati, OH

Gary Ross, PhD
Center for Gerontology
St. Joseph Health System
Flint, MI

Rev. Russell Smith, PhD
Pope John Center
Braintree, MA

Sr. Jacqueline Wagner, O. Carm.
Carmelite Sisters for the Aged & Infirm
Naperville, IL

CHA Staff:

Sr. Diana Bader, OP, PhD
Sr. Juliana Casey, IHM, PhD, STD
Rev. Joseph W. Kukura
Martha M. Morrow
J. Stuart Showalter, JD
Bro. Peter Campbell, JD, CFX
Ellen Newman Geerling
Sr. Elizabeth McMillan, RSM, PhD
Lawrence Seidl
Sr. Teresa Stanley, CCVI, PhD

Special Task Force on Pain Management

John H. Burrows, MD
St. Johns Hospital
Detroit, MI

Margaret Coloney
Center for Hope Hospice
Roselle, NJ

Marilyn Fisher
Cope Center for Pain & Stress Management
Lourdes Hospital
Binghamton, NY

Rev. Lawrence T. Reilly, STD
Sisters of Providence Corporations
Seattle, WA

Alice O'Shaughnessy, MD
Mercy Hospice
Sea Cliff, NY

Suffering and Dying Task Force #1

Barbara Cox
Dominican Health Services
Spokane, WA

Amy Haddad
Center for Health Policy and Ethics
Creighton University
Omaha, NE

T. Patrick Hill
Society for Right to Die/Concern for Dying
New York, NY

Neil Parent
United States Catholic Conference
Washington, DC

Patricia Talone, RSM
St. Helen Convent
Center Square, PA

CHA Staff:

Sr. Diana Bader, OP, PhD
Rev. Joseph W. Kukura
Martha M. Morrow
Bro. Peter Campbell, JD, CFX
Sr. Elizabeth McMillan, RSM, PhD

Suffering and Dying Task Force #2

Joseph P. Costantino
Cardinal Glennon Children's Hospital
St. Louis, MO

William J. Bazan
Catholic Health Association/Wisconsin
Milwaukee, WI

Lori Cappello Dangberg
California Association of Catholic Hospitals
Sacramento, CA

Michael Peters
St. John's Regional Health Center
Springfield, MO

Richard N. McDevitt
New York State Catholic Healthcare Council
Albany, NY

Rev. Michael D. Place, STD
Archdiocese of Chicago
Chicago, IL

Tobias Meeker
St. John's Regional Health Center
Springfield, MO

Sr. Sharon Park, OP
Washington State Catholic Conference
Seattle, WA

CHA Staff:

Sr. Diana Bader, OP, PhD
J. Fred Caesar
Sr. Elizabeth McMillan, RSM, PhD
Martha M. Morrow
Joanne Elden Beale
Rev. Joseph W. Kukura
John Miles, JD

INTRODUCTION

Our contemporary experience with dying reveals our general discomfort with death and with all that surrounds it. Generally, we find it difficult to face a person's death because we are reminded that we, too, will face our own mortality. As long as we live in a world that God has not yet fully redeemed and transformed, we will know suffering and stand in the shadow of death.

Suffering and death are both experiences of loss: suffering may include loss of freedom, loss of physical functioning, loss of mental capacity, and loss of social relationships; death, of course, is loss of life. Since we live as interdependent partners in society, the community also experiences loss when one of its members dies. As St. Paul reminds us, "If one member suffers, all suffer together" (1 Cor 12:26).

People are dying differently today than did persons in earlier centuries. Before the introduction of high-tech medicine, most people died at home surrounded by loved ones in a setting filled with familiar sights, sounds, and smells. Today, more than 80 percent of deaths occur in a healthcare institution where the dying patient is removed from familiar features of life. In such institutional settings, the sophisticated machines often displace the patient as the center of our attention in the dying process. The family is relegated to the sidelines, and sometimes even treated as an intrusion, while busy and efficient healthcare professionals attempt to intervene one more time to prolong life.

We have all heard reports of hopelessly ill patients who lie tethered by tubes to machines employed beyond the point of being beneficial. The machines merely prolong dying. This behavior is prompted, in part, by the mistaken moral conviction that human beings have an obligation to use whatever treatments and technologies are available to prolong physical existence. This behavior is also fueled, in part, by our Promethean culture which lives by the myth of mastery and conquest: We are unwilling to accept defeat or failure. This attitude is reflected by some healthcare professionals who have dedicated their lives to curing illness and therefore may consider their inability to put off death as a defeat.

In view of the heroic efforts made by healthcare professionals to prolong life, many people today fear that their lives will be unreasonably prolonged in a way that adds physical suffering, financial expense, and psychological pain to the most critical moment of their life. Having witnessed long and painful dying and the futile use of life-sustaining treatment for others, more people today have a preoccupation about individual freedom and the rights of patients to exercise self-determination, and many are convinced that the only way in which individuals can be protected from overtreatment is through the legalization of euthanasia and assisted suicide.

The way we care for the dying is influenced by the cultural, political, and clinical contexts in which we live as well as by the theological, moral, and pastoral framework we endorse. This book draws upon the Catholic healthcare tradition as a fundamental resource for caring for the dying in the context of the challenges posed by today's American society. Part I reviews some of the major features in our culture which are influencing our attitudes toward and practices of caring for the dying. Part II considers some of the social and political factors which influence public opinion, debate, and practice on matters pertaining to the way we ought to care for the dying. Part III turns to the clinical context where managing pain is one of the central concerns in caring for the dying. Part IV presents Catholic theological, moral, and pastoral tradition as a base for a principled and virtuous method of caring for the dying in a way that would make euthanasia and assisted suicide unnecessary and unthinkable.

PART I
CULTURAL CONTEXT

Death comes to us all, yet how we experience it, the attitude we take toward it, and the manner in which we care for the dying are highly influenced by the culture in which we are nurtured. This cultural context cannot be ignored when trying to provide and assess adequate care for the dying.

One of the characteristic features of our culture is that the population of those over age 65 is growing more rapidly than the population under 10 years of age. In the early part of this century, the reverse was true. But now, as a result of new technologies, we are able to cure more diseases and repair more injuries than ever before, therefore patients can live longer with a better quality of life. As a result, more people are dying at an older age, and they are dying more slowly.

Furthermore, young people today are more likely to die a quick death. The three leading causes of death for males 15 to 25 years of age are accidents, homicides, and suicides. For females of the same ages, most deaths result from accidents, homicides, and malignancies. AIDS is rapidly rising as the leading cause of death for both males and females between 25 and 45 years of age. The leading causes of death for those over age 65 are heart diseases, strokes, and malignancies. Persons with AIDS and those over age 65 are more likely to die a slow death. The challenge to the healthcare community is to nurture positive attitudes toward death among all ages, and to assist those with terminal illnesses to live well while dying.

To meet this challenge, we must pay attention to at least four significant features of our culture: (1) more people are dying in healthcare institutions rather than in their homes, (2) the ethos of individualism in America, (3) the dominance of technology in medicine, and (4) the pluralistic character of American society.

INSTITUTIONAL DYING

The Shift from the Home to Healthcare Institutions

Not only are more people suffering terminal illnesses and being aware of what is happening to them; more are also dying in some healthcare institution rather than in their homes. Up to 80 percent of reported deaths are estimated to occur in healthcare institutions. This is a notable shift from earlier in this century when the same percentage of deaths occurred in homes. At home the dying person could be surrounded by family and friends and retain a fair amount of control over the dying process. But today, policies and procedures of many hospitals, nursing homes, and extended care facilities severely restrict the dying person's freedom and social contacts. This is especially the case in a hospital's intensive care unit where contact with family and friends is restricted to brief, timed visits and often requires the use of sterile gloves, gowns, masks, and machines. Whatever control the dying person may have had at home has been lost to machines or institutions. The dying person can easily feel out of control and depersonalized in these antiseptic and restricted environments where he or she is often treated as a person recovering from major surgery instead of one whose life is coming to a close. Bringing so many of our dying to hospitals may be a questionable habit, especially since hospitals have become so specialized in fending off death.

Dying in institutions rather than at home also reinforces the reality of denial of death in our society. Most people are shielded from death as a natural fact of human life, unless they have lost a parent or a sibling. The only deaths at home are on television news or police shows, which have an unreality about them. Death happens "out there" to someone else. Many young people have never been to a funeral home, a funeral service, or a nursing home or hospital where they can confront the harsh reality of sickness and death. As long as the living are protected from death, they will not be able to accept the fact of their own inevitable deaths, nor will they see that all lives are limited and thus too precious to waste.

The Shift from Parentalism to Self-Determination

Institutional dying has also resulted in a shift in the roles of caring for the dying. Whereas family and friends were once the primary caregivers, now members of the healthcare professions are. This shift has introduced notable tensions between medical professionals and the patient, including the family, in defining appropriate behavior toward the dying.

One such tension focuses on the power to make decisions. Throughout most of medicine's history, decision making has been dominated by physicians. Since most physicians were male, the term "paternalism" was used to describe this method of determining what options would be provided for the dying and their families. Today we might call the physician-dominated relationship "parentalism." It holds that "Doctor knows best" and leaves little room for patients to participate in making decisions about their own lives. As physicians grew in social status, and as their authority to dispense life and death grew more awesome through the developments of technology, their power over patients became greater.

Today a new twist is occurring in the physician-dominated relationship due to the complex financial climate of healthcare. Once a fee-for-service exchange, medicine now has expanded the traditional physician-patient relationship to include third parties — the government, insurance companies, regulatory agencies, and sometimes even ethics committees. The hospital room is getting crowded!

The physician's claim to authority and control, as well as the claims of bureaucracy, often conflicts with the patient's right to self-determination. The patient's rights movement emerged from the general cultural climate of the 1960s, when all who felt they were subject to oppressive forces were inspired to rise up and demand participation in the decisions that affected them. The living will, the durable power of attorney for healthcare statutes, and the Patient Self-Determination Act of 1991 are all directly in keeping with the goals of this movement to give patients as much control as possible in making decisions which shape their lives.

> The competent patient's informed preferences should be the moral nucleus of the therapeutic relationship.

By respecting the patient's freedom to make these decisions, physicians cannot intervene in the patient's life in any way without the patient's consent. The competent patient's informed preferences, therefore, should be the moral nucleus of the therapeutic relationship. This means that physicians should respect the informed refusal of life-support therapy. For example, when patients show an understanding of the risks and benefits of the proposed treatment weighed in light of their own values and life plans, their decisions to refuse treatment generally should be respected, even if it means hastening death. Some experts estimate that 70 percent of deaths in healthcare institutions are preceded by decisions to forgo life-sustaining treatment. Competent, informed patients should also be allowed to accept or refuse treatment according to their personal values without having such decisions supervised by third parties — the courts, medical societies, insurance agencies, or ethics committees. Paying attention to what patients value about health and life is one way to keep from losing them in the machinery of healthcare bureaucracy and high-tech medicine, which all too often reduce human beings to mere computer appraisals passively subject to physician's orders.

While the great value of supporting the patient's freedom is to uphold the dignity of the human being, its weakness, however, is that an exaggerated sense of personal control over one's life may continue until death. As creatures, we do not have as much control as we might like to think; we are limited by divine sovereignty; as patients, we are constrained by the restrictions of illness, the natural history of disease, and bodily impairment; as social beings, we are not free to do whatever we want without concern for the common good. Yet, an exaggerated sense of freedom and control is fueled by the American bias toward individualism.

INDIVIDUALISM

The American Ethos

Individualism is so much a part of our American heritage that it is one of the most characteristic ways that we distinguish ourselves. An apt metaphor can be found in the story of two hikers in the Rockies who step into a clearing and suddenly encounter a mountain lion poised to pounce. They stop dead in their tracks. One hiker slowly begins to lower his backpack. "Do you really think you can outrun him," asks his friend. "That's not the point," came the reply. "All I have to do is run faster than you."

Individualism disposes each person to look after one's own independent, self-interested goals, owing no one anything and expecting nothing from anyone. The spirit of individualism prizes self-reliance, self-expression, self-direction, and taking charge to ensure that one's own interests are satisfied. Thinking of oneself as apart from being interdependent on others becomes a habit, as does imagining that one's whole destiny lies in one's own hands. No wonder the people who fascinate us and capture our imaginations are the explorer, the pioneer, the entrepreneur, and the self-made man or woman.

This spirit pervades every aspect of our culture. In healthcare, it creates tensions in at least two directions — how to respect a patient's freedom and yet limit his or her autonomy, and how to respect a patient's uniqueness but not isolate him or her from the traditional bonds of the community.

Individualism and Autonomy

We began to feel the effects of the ethos of individualism on healthcare most acutely during the 1960s when many cultural forces converged to re-direct and re-fashion our lives. At that time, the philosophies of existentialism and personalism became more popular and contributed to heightening our awareness that the patient is a person with values and goals, rather than just a body with a disease. The holistic movement grew out of those idealistic concerns for "the patient as a person." If a patient's decisions were to be made solely on the basis of what is medically indicated from a scientific and technical assessment of the diseased state, the physician would be in the best position to decide. But if the person's values, goals, physical and moral resources, social commitments, and desired quality of life are also to be considered in making an appropriate decision, then the patient remains the key decision maker.

In addition, the growth of mass communication has now made medical information available in lay language to a greater extent than ever before. Millions of people have access to information about health matters. No longer are patients insulated from the flow of information about new discoveries for treating certain conditions, about drugs that are available, about procedures that are common or controversial, and about some of the great ethical conflicts in healthcare. Knowledge is power. As a result, many patients have become more sophisticated partners in the therapeutic relationship. Instead of accepting medical decisions unquestioningly, they are more prone to evaluate physicians on the basis of their willingness to enter into a mutually respectful relationship.

The exaggerated autonomy of individualism is the force that has created today's patient-dominated relationship as the typical model for the therapeutic relationship.

The exaggerated autonomy of individualism is the force that has created today's patient-dominated relationship as the typical model for the therapeutic relationship. While the patient must certainly be included in decision making out of respect for his or her dignity as a person, the patient cannot make decisions without help from physicians and other caregivers. The medical relationship needs to be guided by a paradigm of partnership. This ideal model expresses the interdependent nature of the physician's commitment to the patient's welfare and of the patient's dependence on the physician's expertise. Rather than satisfy the self-interests of individualism, the therapeutic relationship must respect the constraints of living interdependently. Multiple relationships — with nurses, therapists, insurers, family, and society in general — are also to be considered, along with the contributions each makes and the implications any choice will have on those relationships.

Autonomy and Euthanasia

The exaggerated autonomy of individualism is one of the basic ideas used to justify arguments for legalized euthanasia and assisted suicide. As the argument goes, by questioning the ethical acceptability of assisted suicide and euthanasia, we question the dignity of human freedom.

The Hemlock Society promotes assisted suicide and euthanasia as the ultimate civil liberties, reflecting a bias toward individualism's libertarian principle, and putting the burden of proof on those who would deprive persons of freedom over their bodies and their lives. The members of that Society feel that human beings have a unique worth because we are free agents. "Death with dignity" easily gets translated by them into something such as: "It's my body; it's my freedom; it's my life; it's my death. Let me have control." According to the libertarian view, killing without permission is what makes taking life wrong, rather than the religiously based conviction that we do not have the right to take life.

The Hemlock Society maintains that persons should be allowed assisted suicide or euthanasia when they choose it freely, and this choice neither violates another's freedom nor is overridden by any restraining duties. Those with a terminal illness best qualify for assisted suicide or euthanasia since they cannot fulfill any further obligations to others; that is, their rights are not overridden by any restraining duties. These rights even extend to eliciting help from healthcare professionals who are committed to helping those in need. The Hemlock Society sees euthanasia and assisted suicide as the ultimate rights of individual freedom because control is retained over one's dying to ensure that a person is not being dependent on others or helpless in the face of technology.

Criticism ot Autonomy

The argument for autonomy, especially the idea of extending the right to self-determination to include the right to be assisted in killing oneself, needs to be critically examined and checked. The bias of those who seek a complete, solitary independence free of constraints is blind to the built-in limits to autonomy. For one thing, a patient's autonomy is necessarily limited by the very definition of a patient. Therefore, the patient is more or less strongly influenced by the internal and external constraints that come with the territory of being sick or dying.

Moreover, our religious convictions tell us that our freedom is limited, especially when it comes to having absolute control over life. We believe that God alone has absolute sovereignty over life and death. The end of human life is not subject to our free determination, but to God's. Human freedom does not extend to choosing the time or conditions for our death. Rather, we exercise our freedom by accepting the limits of living with a perishable body and consenting to our powerlessness in the face of death.

Furthermore, autonomy is limited by the very nature of being human, which includes freedom and life as quintessential elements. Allowing someone else power over our freedom and life, as is the case in euthanasia and assisted suicide, is giving away too much of what it means to be human. In this sense, euthanasia and assisted suicide actually contradict the very freedom and life they claim to respect.

We are also social by nature since we are made in the image of God — a community of loving persons. Because we live in a community of interdependent persons, no one person's freedom is absolute. We cannot do whatever we want. Other people's welfare must also be taken into consideration. The culture of individualism, however, tends to isolate people, creating islands of self-interest where right and wrong become tied to personal preferences.

Freedom means little more than being left alone, especially from what appears to be the arbitrary authority of others — family, church, government, the healthcare establishment. The concept of individualism advocates resolving ethical and public issues in the name of individual liberty rather than thinking about personal desires in relation to the common good.

To treat euthanasia and assisted suicide solely as private acts of personal freedom, then, is a mistake, because they are actually social actions that involve at least one other person. Insofar as the healthcare profession is involved, euthanasia and assisted suicide are private claims on a social good, namely, the good of the healthcare profession committed to serving the broader health needs of others, and not just the preferences of one person. The personal desire to request death from the hand of another, then, ought to be considered a social action, not a private action. And, any effort to sanction it as a practice should be evaluated in light of how it helps or hinders the common good, and not whether it promotes one person's self-interest.

Individualism and Community

To live well while dying, one needs to remain as much in control as possible and to satisfy physical, affective, social, and spiritual needs. These needs are generally met in and through one's primary network of relationships, such as family, friends, and religious and cultural traditions. Securing that network of support is not always easy. The ethos of individualism contributes a fair share to the difficulty.

The same individualism which exalts autonomy also turns upon the person in destructive ways when it inhibits the human bonding that creates the interdependent community that enables individuals to flourish. American individualism can be described by these familiar slogans: "Stand on your own two feet." "Don't burden anyone." "What good are you if you can't do it yourself?" We live by these mottoes and, in some instances die by them, because we so prize independence as a sign of maturity. As adults, we find it difficult to ask for help or to become dependent on anyone, because dependence on others is seen as an unreasonable and burdensome imposition. A self-image nurtured by the rugged individualism of our pioneer spirit will not give us permission to be dependent or a burden. Yet, in reality, we are interdependent already. Rugged individualism is an illusion. We will flourish as individuals only in a nurturing and sharing community.

The ethos of individualism, then, poses a serious challenge to caring for the dying. How are we to balance the dying person's need for independence, whereby he or she can feel respect and exercise freedom, with their need to be part of other people's lives, where they can feel loved and cherished and truly flourish? To enable the terminally ill to live well while dying, we need to allow them to retain as much control as possible within the limits of belonging to a community. Also, we need to secure their network of significant relationships (their "family") so that they can experience the affective bonds of trust and love which support personal dignity and enhance the meaning of life. Designing appropriate caring interventions should neither deny the dying freedom nor isolate them from the living.

TECHNOLOGY

An American Medical Standard

The powerful presence of technology in medicine is another characteristic of today's culture. In fact, the medical industry has become a symbol of technological achievement. The American way of delivering healthcare is distinguished by an extraordinary reliance on technology as the instrument for helping people. We seek technological control over nature from womb to tomb.

The availability and ready reliance on technology is a good news/bad news story. The good news is that technological advances in healthcare have certainly created new opportunities for curing illnesses and prolonging life. No one wants to roll back the clock to earlier days and lose the efficiency with which technology can aid diagnosis and treatment. But what price are we paying for its use? Therein lies the bad news. Technology fuels the myth that we are a Promethean society. We believe we can solve every problem, conquer every disease, and control every contingency if we work at it long enough and develop the right instruments. We do not take well to inevitable defeat. Our successes set up the expectation that we will discover even more. This passion for progress, mastery, and control through technological achievement discourages us from facing our limits and subjects us to the tyranny of technological domination.

An increased interest in legalizing euthanasia and assisted suicide correlates with the increased fear many people have of being trapped in unacceptable conditions of dependency and disability brought about by medicine's power to prolong dying by means of machines taking over every vital function in the body.

The Technological Imperative

Just having medical technology around creates a mindset that technologies that can be developed ought to be developed; and, if we have it, we ought to use it. Available technology becomes part of standard treatment, even if its use on a particular patient may create more burdens than benefits. For example, some physicians find it difficult not to use dialysis machines, ventilators, or feeding tubes even when they only prolong dying. Similarly, some patients and families find it hard to refuse them since technology represents the best standard of care. To shift away from its use represents, perhaps, a lower quality of care or the potential abuse of undertreatment. The sentiment created by having so much technology around is that not to use the latest technology is to "miss out" on the best medicine can offer. Because some persons benefit from its use, then all patients become subject to it. Some simply find it difficult to accept that medical treatment can be too burdensome or futile. Thus, available technologies end up overwhelming human freedom rather than enhancing it.

The availability of technology has raised questions about its appropriate use. In a society that is captivated by science and its awesome results and efficiency, we can easily lose sight of the overall purpose to be served by technology. Medical technology is to be used in service of the total good of the patient. This includes not only the relief or cure that therapy can bring, but also what the patient prefers, values about life, and regards as giving ultimate meaning to life. Achieving only relief or prolonging physical life by means of technological assistance does not necessarily benefit the total good of the patient.

The temptation to be dominated by technological equipment stands in opposition to the unrecognized wisdom that not everything that can be done ought to be done. This is the wisdom that hopes to avoid another form of oppression of the weak and dependent by the healthy and powerful. This is also the wisdom that is firmly based on the long-standing principle that requires the use of only ordinary treatment, that is, treatment which brings a benefit proportionate to the burdens the patient would have to bear as a result. We will see more of this wisdom and principle in Part IV.

Available technologies end up overwhelming human freedom rather than enhancing it.

The Primacy of the Person

The threat of depersonalization makes guarding against the pressure of technological domination so critical for the appropriate care of the dying. Our reliance on technology can too easily become a substitute for the healing touch of human interpersonal relationships. For example, physicians can now diagnose and prescribe medicine on the basis of data provided by machines, which means, in some instances, they never have to see or touch the patient. Also, machines often come between the caregiver and the patient so that the patient no longer feels like an independent person, but rather, an extension of the machine. In such a setting, a patient can easily lose the sense of personal identity, dignity, independence, and control over the direction of his or her life.

Legalized euthanasia or assisted suicide may become attractive as a means to avoid such an indignity from ever happening, or a means to escape once it occurs.

Healthcare professionals whose identities have been fashioned out of a ministry of person-to-person healing must be made aware of the risk of depersonalizing care for the dying. The availability of technology can too easily reduce healing to fixing. Fixing treats bodies as interconnected parts, while healing treats the person holistically as a multidimensional being with physical, emotional, intellectual, social, and spiritual needs. The challenge of so much technology is to transform the stethoscope and scalpel, the sonogram and MRI into a type of human touch. Only when healthcare professionals have a larger concern for the whole person and a concern that the meaning of the patient's life reaches beyond merely biological existence, then medical technology can be made subject to the total good of the patient rather than making the patient subject to the power of technology.

AMERICAN PLURALISM

Another feature of our culture which influences care for the dying is the multicultural context in which care must be delivered. One's cultural traditions influence not only *how* something is talked about, but even *if* it is talked about at all, especially such matters as dying and death. Protocols established by our healthcare institutions to enhance service must reflect an awareness of these cultural patterns. For example, our desire to be efficient may overtly or subtly threaten to replace the religious and family traditions which are so much a part of the multicultural groups which make up American society. These protocols can too easily deprive the dying person of those powerfully symbolic expressions of meaning, love, and hope which come from a religious, ethnic, national, or familial tradition. Care for the dying is impoverished if the patient's cultural context and resources are ignored and he or she is treated as simply a technical problem.

The Catholic healthcare institution today is challenged, therefore, to reconcile two profoundly difficult tasks: first, to affirm what is important in the Catholic tradition; and second, to respect the diversity of the social and religious values of those who work and are cared for in the institution.

No one has a ready prescription to cure these complex conflicts. Those who feel the tension inherent in these tasks will inevitably have to draw upon their creative imaginations to resolve them. Healthcare professionals will need courage and humility to affirm their own faith while respecting the diversity that is around them. The Catholic healthcare institution must strive to promote a sensitivity and respect for cultural diversity regarding care for the dying. Sensitivity begins by welcoming the expression of cultural diversity and by promising to respect differences. No one should ever be asked to violate deeply held moral convictions. When cultural differences clash with moral convictions and reconciliation seems impossible, the parties involved in conflict should be disengaged with as little disruption as possible. Catholic institutions should implement policies, educational programs, mission effectiveness committees, and ethics committees to promote and protect the multicultural dimensions of the care of the dying.

> The Catholic healthcare institution must strive to promote a sensitivity and respect for cultural diversity regarding care for the dying.

Conclusion

Part I has reviewed some of several cultural factors and their implications which influence the care we give to the dying. We need to pay attention to their influences on us if we are to fashion attitudes and actions that will yield not only compassionate care for the dying, but also give clear Catholic witness to the dignity and value of the person at every stage of life.

Implications for Catholic Healthcare

◆ Today people are living longer and dying more slowly. How do we nurture positive attitudes toward death as a part of life in order to enable everyone to live well while dying?

◆ Today more people die in healthcare institutions than in family homes. What are we doing to enable patients to remain, as much as possible, in control of the decisions which affect their living and dying?

◆ The competent patient's informed choices are the moral nucleus of the therapeutic relationship. How do we promote and honor such documents as advance directives to ensure informed consent and respect for the patient's decisions on the use of life-prolonging treatments?

◆ The ethos of individualism advocates exaggerated autonomy. How do we provide examples of our human interdependence? Do we work toward securing a therapeutic relationship of partnership? Do we help balance personal wishes with the common good?

◆ Individuals can flourish in a nurturing and sharing community. In our care for dying persons, how do we work to secure their network of significant relationships so that they can experience the affective bonds of trust and love which support personal dignity and enhance the meaning of life?

◆ Technology is pervasive in the delivery of healthcare today. Do we critically examine our use of technology in order to avoid losing the healing touch of the person-to-person relationship? Do we keep the use of technology subject to the total good of the patient?

◆ In the multicultural society of America, how do we foster familiarity with and respect for the dying person's cultural context and resources of religious, ethnic, national, or familial traditions which provide expressions of meaning, love, and hope to sustain the patient?

PART II

SOCIAL AND POLITICAL CONTEXT

The increased level of activity in state legislatures and courts of law regarding "natural death" and the "right to die" demands that the social and political dimensions of issues about the end of life also be addressed. A developing "war of words" in today's society threatens to refashion our understanding of death, dying, and refusing treatment; therefore, a correct understanding of major terms is key. The first part of this section will aim to clarify the value-laden words most frequently used in the media and in public debates on issues about the end of life. The second part of this section will discuss the way these issues are being handled in the legislative arena, the media, the courts, and healthcare institutions.

TERMS

Terms mean different things to different people. It is not surprising, then, that we may ultimately find ourselves talking past one another when we use the same words. Therefore, clarifying the terms used in public debate is necessary if we are to avoid fundamental misunderstandings and speak a common language about how best to care for patients at the end of life.

Legislators, media personnel, and even, at times, religious authorities do not always appreciate the complexity of the issues and the potential for misunderstanding by the public. Vague and emotionally charged words about decisions to refuse treatment at the end of life are characteristic of groups who at times appear to use terms as slogans to promote a particular political agenda. Unhappily, this lack of clarity about key terms leads to confusion about important values. A clear and consistent use of terms is crucial if agents of public influence — media, legislatures, courts, and healthcare institutions themselves — are to have a positive role in the development of societal values, norms, and policies affecting the way we care for the dying.

Death

Most state laws defining death now reflect the requirements listed in the Uniform Determination of Death Act: "An individual who has sustained either (1) irreversible cessation of circulatory and respiratory functions, or (2) irreversible cessation of all functions of the entire brain, including the brain stem, is dead. A determination of death must be made in accordance with accepted medical standards."

In recent years, proposals to revise the brain criteria for determining death have been debated vigorously among doctors, lawyers, and ethicists. The proposed revision, called "cerebral" or "neocortical" death, would determine death on the basis of "the irreversible cessation of those brain functions necessary to sustain any level of consciousness." However, "neocortical" (or "cerebral") death is not to be confused with brain death, which is defined as the total cessation of all functions of the entire brain. In the *Karen Quinlan* case, for example, the U.S. Supreme Court ruled that the patient was "cerebrally dead" but not brain dead. While the debate continues, the only acceptable criteria for determining death at this time are those for *whole brain* death.

It is of utmost importance to have a clear agreement on what constitutes death so that we do not treat the dead as though they were alive, nor the living as though dead. The living may still require life-sustaining treatment. But when a person has died, all treatment ought to cease. The key moral question in these debates centers on whether "neocortical death" or "brain death" is more consistent with an adequate understanding of human life, and thus, human death.

Death with Dignity

This is dying in a way which is not unduly burdened by the prolonged use of life-sustaining technology in an alienating and depersonalizing environment. From a Catholic perspective, the dignity of the person derives from his or her relationship with God. Dying with dignity is continuous with living with dignity. Death is a passage every person inevitably must face to enter the fullness of his or her relationship with God.

Everyone has the obligation to help ease the passage and to accompany the dying person until the end, but there is no obligation to use every available means to prolong life in every situation.

An incorrect use of the term "death with dignity" would be as a slogan to romanticize death or to promote the so-called "right to die."

Right To Die

This is a curious way to refer to a natural inevitability. The "right" at stake here is not to die, but to make the request for euthanasia or assisted suicide.

American law does not recognize a constitutionally protected right to die. The U.S. Supreme Court did recognize in the *Cruzan*[1] case an individual's "liberty interest" in refusing unwanted medical treatment. According to the Court, this interest can be limited by procedural safeguards designed to protect the state's interest in preserving life and to ensure that others act in conformity with the patient's wishes.

The Catholic Church opposes an absolute "right to die." The Catholic tradition values a person's self-determination in making medical decisions, including the refusal of life-sustaining measures, as one of the most basic expressions of the dignity of the person. However, the Catholic moral tradition limits this right to refuse treatment based on a moral order which requires human beings to act as responsible stewards of their lives and health, and not as absolute arbiters about their ultimate destiny. Catholic teaching advocates a lesser emphasis on individual autonomy and freedom of choice that are so prized in the American ethos.

Euthanasia

An authoritative definition according to official Catholic teaching is "an action or an omission which of itself or by intention causes death, in order that all suffering may in this way be eliminated" (Vatican *Declaration on Euthanasia*[2], 1980). An authoritative legal definition of euthanasia is "the act or practice of painlessly putting to death persons suffering from incurable and distressing disease as an act of mercy" (*Black's Law Dictionary*[3]). Within a common law tradition, such as we have in the U.S. legal system, definitions evolve from cases. Although legal definitions have moral content, they are accepted by society as a reflection of law, not morality. Therefore, we should not assume that Black's legal definition constitutes a moral endorsement of euthanasia as a practice; it merely describes a practice that then needs to be evaluated legally and morally by all members of that society.

Catholic teaching advocates a lesser emphasis on individual autonomy and freedom of choice that are so prized in the American ethos.

Of the many classifications that have been given to euthanasia, two key dimensions prevail. The first relates to the degree of consent to euthanasia (voluntary or involuntary), and the second relates to the form by which it is carried out (active or passive). Euthanasia is *active* and *voluntary* when a person explicitly requests help to die and a lethal injection, for example, is then given. It is *involuntary* and *active* when directed toward a person who is incapable of making a request to die (such as an infant, a young child, a mentally retarded person, or a comatose patient) but whose proxy (such as a parent, spouse, guardian, or physician) makes the request and makes certain that the lethal procedure is carried out. Neither of these forms of active euthanasia is morally acceptable.

Passive euthanasia, on the other hand, is a much more confusing term. It can be morally acceptable or unacceptable with or without the patient's consent. It is unacceptable when omitting a medical procedure or protocol which one has a duty to perform, when that omission intentionally ends a life. For example, refusing to repair an intestinal blockage in a newborn with Down's syndrome is unacceptable passive euthanasia. However, "passive euthanasia" is morally acceptable when it means omitting a medical intervention which is futile and/or too burdensome for the patient, thus allowing the patient to die from natural causes; such as withdrawing a respirator from an irreversibly comatose person with end-stage brain cancer. This form of passive euthanasia is acceptable because the intention is not to take the person's life, but to allow the person to die without burdensome treatment.

The term "passive euthanasia" can unfortunately be misleading; it may be confused with the concept of withholding and withdrawing futile and/or burdensome treatment, or it may too easily be generalized to suggest positive connotations for all forms of euthanasia. Therefore, we may be better off not using this term at all.

Killing/Allowing To Die

Closely related to the concept of euthanasia, and thus often associated with the active/passive distinction, are the terms killing and allowing to die. The Catholic medical-moral tradition maintains the moral difference between them. This moral difference lies behind the *ordinary/extraordinary means* standard used to guide decisions to treat or not to treat.

"Killing" refers to a human agent being morally responsible for causing death. We can rightly say that a physician "kills" the patient, if, for example, the physician intervenes with a lethal injection, or withholds or withdraws treatment which should be provided because it is reasonable to do so. But "killing" does not properly apply to the action of wthholding or withdrawing treatment that is unreasonable because it is burdensome or no longer beneficial. "Allowing to die" more accurately expresses the moral reality of this action.

"Allowing to die" refers to stopping treatment which is burdensome or offers no reasonable hope of benefit so that the underlying pathology, which called for the use of the treatment in the first place, will run its course and eventually cause the patient's death. In such an instance, no one is morally responsible for the death since the fatal pathology causes the death.

The distinction between killing and allowing to die is best retained in euthanasia debates because it differentiates deaths for which we are morally responsible from those for which we are not. This distinction protects the overall respect for life because it recognizes that human beings are limited in their ability to control the ultimate progression of a fatal disease, and it preserves the social role of the physician as committed to curing and caring rather than to killing.

Mercy Killing

"Mercy killing" is another name for euthanasia. It is used to emphasize that persons who request euthanasia do so to escape the physical and mental suffering that may accompany the terminal stages of a fatal disease. Also, it suggests that persons who commit euthanasia do so out of compassion for the victim and to end the victim's pain and suffering.

According to the Vatican *Declaration on Euthanasia*[4], "mercy killing" is killing "for the purpose of putting an end to extreme suffering, or saving abnormal babies, the mentally ill, or the incurably sick from the prolongation, perhaps for many years, of a miserable life, which could impose too heavy a burden on their families and society."

Black's Law Dictionary[5] defines "mercy killing" as follows: "Euthanasia. The affirmative act of bringing about immediate death allegedly in a painless way and generally administered by one who thinks that the dying person wishes to die because of a terminal or hopeless disease or condition."

The Catholic moral tradition rejects suicide as a way to escape prolonged and barely tolerable pain.

Suicide

Suicide is the intentional and deliberate taking of one's own life. According to *Black's Law Dictionary*[6], it is "self-destruction. The deliberate termination of one's own life." Most state laws have decriminalized suicide, but public safety officials in every municipality intervene as a matter of course to prevent individuals from committing suicide.

The Catholic moral tradition rejects suicide as a way to escape prolonged and barely tolerable pain. The Church, however, refrains from passing judgment on someone who resorts to suicide in desperation.

Some "right-to-die" advocates have coined the terms "self-deliverance" and "exiting" to refer to suicide.

Assisted Suicide (Aid-in-Dying)

Although suicide is decriminalized, in most states helping someone to commit suicide is treated as criminal homicide. "Homicide" is defined by *Black's Law Dictionary*[7] as "the killing of one human being by the act, procurement, or omission of another." It is a crime only if done with criminal intent. The Hemlock Society, through its political arm Americans Against Suffering, is attempting to decriminalize assisted suicide.

The term "aid-in-dying" conceals more than it reveals. All sorts of "aid" can be given to the dying, such as companionship, love, and appropriate pain management; but the term is not being used to mean these types of aid. Recently used in efforts to legalize assisted suicide, "aid-in-dying" refers to physicians taking steps to help terminally ill patients commit suicide by providing the means and the knowledge of how to take one's own life. The Michigan cases involving Dr. Jack Kevorkian, who helped patients self-administer a lethal dose of drugs by using an intravenous mechanism or by inhaling a lethal gas, are notorious examples of assisted suicide or aid-in-dying.

The Vatican *Declaration on Euthanasia* is clear in its moral evaluation of assisted suicide: "No one is permitted to ask for this act of killing, either for self or for another person entrusted to his or her care, nor can one consent to it, either explicitly or implicitly. Nor can any authority legitimately recommend or permit such an action. For it is a question of the violation of the divine law, an offense against the dignity of the human person, a crime against life, and an attack on humanity."

Persistent Vegetative State

A persistent vegetative state (PVS) occurs with the functional loss of the cerebral hemispheres of the brain, which control consciousness, awareness, and other voluntary and involuntary actions. However, in PVS the functions controlled by the brain stem continue, such as respiration and the primitive reflex of pupillary response to light and the cough and gag reflexes. Patients in a persistent vegetative state may exhibit many normal brain-stem functions, such as periods of wakefulness and sleep, eye movement, pupillary response, spontaneous respiration, and protective cough and gag reflexes; however, they are completely unconscious and unaware of their environment and exhibit no voluntary reactions or responses. Put simply, they are awake but unaware.

In contrast, *coma* is a state of unconsciousness in which a person does not have sleep-wake cycles and exhibits no voluntary reactions or responses. The person in a coma appears to be asleep.

A few dramatic cases of patients "waking up" after a long period of apparently permanent unconsciousness have been widely and somewhat sensationally reported in the media, suggesting to some that life-support should never be withheld. Physicians, however, have questioned whether these few patients were accurately diagnosed from the beginning as permanently unconscious.

These are only a few of the commonly used terms in the public debate on issues pertaining to the end of life. Careful use of these terms can only help clear up some of the confusion that makes dialogue on these issues so difficult.

PUBLIC OPINION AND THE MEDIA

Opinion Polls

In the wake of Janet Adkins' death by Dr. Kevorkian's "suicide machine," a *New York Times*/CBS News poll (1990) surveyed Americans on their reaction. Fifty-three percent said "yes" when asked whether a doctor should be allowed to help someone in Adkins' situation to take his or her life. In the same year, a *Los Angeles Times* national poll found 55 percent of those surveyed supported a patient's right to commit suicide if he or she is suffering without hope of improvement. Some of the survey respondents considered suicide in this situation to be justifiable in the sense that it was understandable, but not acceptable as public policy.

Opinion polls over the past two decades have shown a steady increase in popular support for euthanasia and assisted suicide. In May, 1990, the Times Mirror Center for People and the Press, based in Washington, DC, conducted a national telephone survey of the public on related issues surrounding the end of life. They compared their results with those of similar surveys done over the last 20 years. Their analysis showed an increase in public support for the patient's right to choose and for the use of proxies as decision makers. The results also noted a trend toward a greater acceptance of suicide in the face of suffering from a terminal disease.

Surveys such as these both reflect and create social attitudes and values about issues pertaining to the end of life and to the care of the dying. However, the statistics should be examined with caution. While national polls sometimes create the impression of a great deal of homogeneity in attitudes and opinions, in fact, real differences do exist but fail to show up because of how questions are asked or how data are analyzed. Another concept to be weighed is the impact of influential industries on regional public attitudes. For example, since major news networks are in the Northeast (although Atlanta has become increasingly important in recent years), this section of the country influences to a great extent the public information broadcast about events such as Dr. Kevorkian's "death machine." Also, the entertainment industry, primarily based in southern California, exerts influence in shaping public attitudes on these questions through television and films.

The entertainment industry, primarily based in southern California, exerts influence in shaping public attitudes on these questions through television and films.

Mass Media

Increasingly, medical and ethical issues surrounding the end of life are appearing in news stories, in feature articles in popular magazines, in best-selling books, and on national television. Even more common are television dramas which depict anguishing decisions about forgoing and discontinuing medical treatment and taking one's own life. One of these programs, *Last Wish*, portrayed the story of how Betty Rollin helped her mother suffering from ovarian cancer to commit suicide.

The success of Derek Humphry's best-selling how-to book on effective suicide, *Final Exit: The Practicalities of Self-Deliverance and Assisted Suicide for the Dying*[8], fills people's consciousness with a new meaning for a "good death" (the English translation of the Greek "euthanasia"). This book advocates using such means as plastic bags and poisons to bring about one's own death without the agony of decline, pain, or dependence on others. Its popularity is a strong indictment of healthcare systems that fail to control pain and fail to provide emotional, social, and spiritual support.

By acknowledging the influence of the media in forming attitudes and opinions, healthcare institutions can seize opportunities for public education on fundamental human and religious values. To influence public opinion through the media on issues surrounding the end of life, the first effort has to be directed toward educating the members of the media themselves. Only then is it possible to work with and through them to reach the public. Some strategies for informing the media are to host regular meetings for media leaders, to offer to serve as an informative resource, to host public debates on important and controversial issues, and to meet with medical reporters to discuss issues such as those covered in this book.

THE LEGISLATIVE FRAMEWORK

Legislation on Advance Directives

Legislative debates over the past five to ten years have centered on ways to enable individuals to exercise their right to refuse treatment more effectively without compromising the interests of the state in protecting life. In the wake of California's Natural Death Act, passed in 1976, most states have enacted legislation regarding both the living will and the durable power of attorney for healthcare. Current debates focus on such issues as educating patients to know their right to refuse treatment, on determining the role of the surrogate decision maker, and on allowing the withdrawal of medically assisted nutrition and hydration. Other debates, as seen in legislative initiatives on the West Coast, center on the legalization of euthanasia and physician-assisted suicide.

The common-law tradition of informed consent is the basis for more recent legislation protecting a patient's right to refuse unwanted treatments. In virtually every state the existence of refusal-of-treatment legislation, such as laws regarding the living will and durable power of attorney for healthcare, suggests that many people feel that they have lost control over making decisions about medical treatment for themselves or their loved ones. The enactment of these laws also suggests that physicians feel that they may need protection when acting on the request of their patients to limit or to stop treatment.

Most of the legislative activity has been at the state level. However, a federal law, the Patient Self-Determination Act, became law December 1, 1991. It requires all healthcare facilities receiving Medicare funds to: (1) provide patients with information about their rights to accept or refuse treatment and to make an advance directive, (2) maintain written policies and procedures to ensure that patients receive such information in written form, (3) document on the patient's medical record whether the patient has executed an advance directive, and (4) provide both staff and the community education about advance directives.

Lawyers have warned the public that there is no fail-safe method to assure that one's wishes regarding treatment will be honored if a person should become incompetent. The advantage of advance directives is that they are usually very valuable indicators of a person's preferences. Sample forms are now readily available from healthcare organizations and through citizen advocacy organizations, such as the American Association of Retired Persons. Advance directives are, however, only a means to an end. Their greatest benefit is to provide an opportunity for people to express their values and the ways they would expect those values to be honored in decisions about their medical treatment, and to discuss these details with family members, close friends, and their physician.

Some Catholic moral theologians and Church authorities were initially opposed to living wills because they saw them as a potential threat to the fundamental moral rights of those who have not executed a living will. They thought that by endorsing living wills, the Church would be saying that the right to refuse treatment could *only* be exercised through the living will document. But when it became evident that patients needed statutory protection from life-prolonging treatment that they did not want or need, the Church recognized the value of formal advance directives. The Catholic Church supports the concept of an advance directive; however, it would oppose the request for euthanasia or assisted suicide and the request to do everything regardless of cost in order to keep a physical organism alive. Neither extreme is acceptable.

When it became evident that patients needed statutory protection from life-prolonging treatment that they did not want or need, the Church recognized the value of formal advance directives.

In the context of so much high-tech medicine, Catholics should be encouraged to fill out an advance directive since it may be the most effective way to exercise stewardship over one's life and health. Catholic healthcare providers should regard these documents as instruments to help them communicate more effectively with patients about their wishes. The process through which the advance directive is developed and discussed with physician, family, and close friends can be one of the most meaningful ways to stimulate reflection on the values of the Catholic tradition.

Proxy Decisions

Legislation on advance directives raises the issue of the role of the proxy or surrogate decision maker. The role of the surrogate is to represent the expressed wishes or, when those are not known, the best interests of the patient for whom he or she speaks. Some states limit the scope of the surrogate's authority to make certain decisions, such as prohibiting a surrogate to withdraw medically provided fluids and nutrition. Typically a surrogate designated by the patient in a durable power of attorney document, for example, has greater authority than family members who are not so formally designated. But without such formal designation, healthcare institutions and legal organizations tend to defer to close family members to communicate the wishes of an incompetent or incapacitated patient.

Goals of Legislation

The ideal legislative framework balances the rights of the patient (and his or her surrogate), the conscience of healthcare providers, and the interests of the state. The fundamental patient right that needs to be protected is that of self-determination or autonomy. But patients also need to be protected from neglect or abuse by healthcare providers and others who may withhold beneficial treatment. The state is empowered to act on their behalf. The interests of the state traditionally enumerated are: (1) protecting life, (2) preventing suicide, (3) protecting the interests of innocent third parties, and (4) safeguarding the integrity of the medical profession.

In 1985, the Committee for Pro-Life Activities of the National Conference of Catholic Bishops (NCCB) published *Guidelines for Legislation on Life-Sustaining Treatment*[9] to serve as a kind of ethical blueprint for the evaluation of emerging legislation on decisions about treatment. In 1986, the same office published a statement on *Uniform Rights of the Terminally Ill Act*[10] drafted by the National Conference of Commissioners on Uniform State Laws. In both of these public statements, the NCCB expressed concern that legislation reflect:

- An emphasis on the societal interest in preserving life, preventing suicide and homicide, and protecting the integrity of the medical profession
- Some limits to the immunities given providers who withdraw life-sustaining treatment

- A presumption in favor of continuing nutrition and hydration to sustain life, while recognizing exceptional circumstances (See also "Nutrition and Hydration: Moral and Pastoral Reflections"[11] issued by the Committee for Pro-Life Activities, April 1992.)
- Provisions that encourage communication among patient, family, and physician
- Protection for the unborn child of a terminally ill mother.

The latter document also urged that there be an open public debate before decisions are made to limit the amount of funds available in certain healthcare settings.

Legislative support for patient self-determination can be a positive step to encourage patients to participate in decisions about their medical treatment.

Decriminalizing physician-assisted suicide, however, will predictably produce more harm than good. If such an option were available, serious abuses may occur because of the social and cultural inequities that exist in U.S. healthcare. For example, dying patients could choose active interventions to end their lives because of pressures arising from lack of financial or emotional support in dying. Further, vulnerable and incompetent patients might be assisted in terminating life as a solution to the economic and other burdens of caring for a growing elderly and chronically ill population. Finally, we have no guarantee that our judicial system would not mandate that physicians must advise patients of a constitutional right to physician-assisted suicide, thus influencing patient's choices because of physician pressure, even if unconscious and unintended.

Specific Catholic theological and moral principles and perspectives for opposing euthanasia and assisted suicide will be detailed in Part IV of this book.

ROLE OF THE COURTS

The role of the courts is to provide a forum for adjudicating conflicts between the rights of individuals and state interests, as well as those conflicts arising between parties over respective rights and liabilities. The patient's right to consent to or refuse treatment is the background for judicial deliberation.

Some cases regarding the right to refuse treatment have been decided on the basis of a state or so-called federal "right to privacy." Other courts, disputing the existence of this constitutional right to privacy, have nevertheless ruled on behalf of an individual's right to refuse treatment on the basis of a "liberty interest." In several cases, notably *Cruzan*[12] in Missouri and *O'Connor*[13] in New York, the state court has ruled in favor of the state's interest in preserving life and requires "clear and convincing" evidence (such as would be found in a written advance directive) from the patient before permitting the withholding or withdrawing of life-sustaining treatment.

The degree to which the court should be active in resolving decisions about treatment is an issue of great importance. Put simply, the issue is whether the court should be making decisions that should rightfully be made by the patient (or by his or her surrogate). Patient self-determination, then, is properly exercised when the patient (or surrogate), in consultation with the physician, decides what is best. Programs provided by healthcare ethics committees or pastoral care staffs can also help support the primary decision maker and, if necessary, mediate conflicts.

Another concern about the role of the courts is their relationship to the legislature. Ideally, the court renders judgment within a legal framework that gives sufficient weight to the public interest. However, state laws reflect not only the public mores in a particular state or region, but considerable political maneuvering by special interest groups as well. What is truly in the public interest is most likely to be achieved if public debate is informed, vigorous, and widely participative.

ROLE OF HEALTHCARE INSTITUTIONS

Healthcare institutions have an indispensable role in facilitating private and public moral discussion on questions of refusing treatment. Since most deaths occur in these institutions, they are the places where most of the decisions in question are made. While healthcare institutions strive to be caring communities, unfortunately people are often alienated by institutional policies and the patterns of practice of physicians and the nursing staff. This environment fosters the imperative to treat at all costs; it may inadvertently create public sympathy with the slogans, "right to die" and "death with dignity."

No one denies that healthcare institutions are operating within serious constraints: medical staff may be inclined to use more rather than less technology; reimbursement policies may channel disproportionate amounts of resources to acute interventions at the expense of preventive and chronic care; financial liability for malpractice continues to increase; government Medicare funding continues to decrease; "market incentives" may be prompted to attract patients with "high ticket" ailments; and nursing staff shortages remain.

Healthcare institutions have significant opportunities to assume a leadership role in transforming current policy and practice into ways of making decisions about treatment that are more humane and dignified. For example, institutional administrators need to recognize the limitation of resources. If healthcare institutions are effectively to support the right and responsibility of patients to guide the course of their own treatment, administrators must make sure their staff understands the issues and that informed staff members are in place to help patients and families act responsibly to come to terms with the limits imposed by sickness and ultimately death.

Even in a supportive environment, however, some patients may make requests that are inconsistent with the policies of the healthcare institution. In such cases, the institution must carefully balance its right to act in accord with its mission and expressed values with the right of the individual to have his or her wishes honored. The patient's right to refuse treatment is not absolute. However, the institution has the duty to show good reason for not honoring the patient's wishes. This is especially important in those cases when the institution has no explicit public policy that would alert patients to an institutionally imposed limitation on their right to refuse treatment.

Finally, healthcare institutions can play an important role independently or through national and state associations by advocating legislative structures that foster an appropriate balance between protecting a patient's right to self-determination and the state's interests to protect life. At the same time, their advocacy should demand sufficient resources for holistic care for the dying.

The media continues to influence public opinion in the way it portrays and accents different features of the experience of dying.

Conclusion

The social and political issues pertaining to appropriate care for the dying are complex. Key terms are poorly understood and often reduced to slogans. This only aggravates the tension in public debates and confuses public discussion. Sometimes we do not realize what we are for or against because we mean different things by the same terms. The media continues to influence public opinion in the way it portrays and accents different features of the experience of dying. Legislation on these matters is uneven and still being developed. The courts have had a greater hand in making medical decisions than most would want them to have. Healthcare institutions ultimately must assert more influence by encouraging patients to make responsible decisions about the limits of their treatment. Above all, Catholic healthcare institutions need to become ideal examples of a caring community, where patients and caregivers enable each other to confront the fear of death and find support in living with loss and human limitation. The final section of this book will elaborate on this need, since public demands for euthanasia and assisted suicide are in part an expression of people's fears of abandonment and isolation in an institution.

Implications for Catholic Healthcare

◆ Because the major terms used in the public debate are understood in different ways, how careful are we to avoid using slogans and to be clear about the meaning of key terms that express important values?

◆ Public opinion is strongly influenced by the media and by the way questions are asked in polls. How critical are we of claims to homogeneity in attitudes and opinions?

◆ News stories, television dramas, popular magazine articles, and "how-to" suicide manuals have captured the attention of the public. What are we doing to educate members of the media about these issues?

◆ As federal and state legislation mandating advance directives has expanded, what are we doing to educate the community about advance directives, and to educate caregivers about respecting the preferences expressed in these documents?

◆ The courts have frequently become involved in decisions that should be made by the patient or proxy after dialogue with the physician. In order to avoid unnecessary recourse to the courts, what effective means do we provide within the healthcare institution to support the primary decision makers and to mediate conflicts?

◆ In face of the fact that most deaths occur in healthcare institutions, how successfully do we do the following: (1) transform current policy and practice into ways of making decisions about treatment that are more respectful of human dignity; (2) provide trained staff who can help patients and families to act responsibly; and (3) advocate legislative structures that foster a balance between protecting the patient's self-interest and the common good?

PART III
CLINICAL CONTEXT

Thus far, we have considered the general cultural context and the social/political realities which influence our attitudes and practices toward caring for the dying. This section will discuss the factors in the clinical setting where most deaths occur.

Many who care for the dying tell us that people are generally not afraid to die. They fear, rather, the process of dying, especially the dependency, helplessness, and pain that so often accompany terminal illness. One of the primary purposes of medicine in caring for the dying should be the relief of pain and the suffering caused by it. While physical pain is the most common source of suffering, pain in dying extends beyond the physical; therefore, effectively managing pain in all its forms is critical in the appropriate care of the dying.

One of the major arguments of euthanasia advocates is that for some people dying is too painful to endure and so bringing about death by lethal injection or assisted suicide is the only merciful way to end the pain and suffering. Our healthcare institutions can have a great influence on the euthanasia movement if we strive to be successful in relieving pain. This section will consider aspects of managing both the physical pain and the psycho-social-spiritual pain that often accompany terminal illness.

PAIN

Pain most often has four different components: physical, psychological, social, and spiritual.

Physical Pain

Physical pain is the most obvious and the major cause of suffering. It arises from injury, disease, or from the general deterioration of the body in the elderly and the terminally ill and impairs physical functioning, mood, and social interaction. At the physical level, pain functions as a clear warning that something is out of order in the normal functioning of the body. But since pain affects the whole person, it can easily exceed its function as a warning signal. Severe pain can drive a person urgently to request its removal at any price, even to the point of asking for death for oneself or obtaining death for others.

Psycho-Social-Spiritual Pain

Psychological pain often arises from facing the inevitability of death, losing control over the process of dying, letting go of hopes and dreams, or having to redefine the world one is about to leave in terms that never quite satisfy one's needs. Psychological pain is evident in mood swings and in the experience of strong feelings which often accompany terminal illness.

Social pain is the pain of isolation, which arises from being forced to reshape relationships. The difficulty of communicating what one is experiencing while dying creates a sense of aloneness at a time when companionship is most needed. The unwillingness or inability of others to keep company with the dying by visiting them, by listening to their feelings and experiences, or by discussing the implications of what is happening to them, only aggravates the isolation. The loss of a familiar social role is also painful. For example, a dying parent becomes dependent on the children and acquiesces to being cared for by them. Letting go of the role of being the self-sufficient, caring parent and becoming the one who is dependent and cared for is painful.

Spiritual pain arises from a loss of meaning, purpose, and hope. Despite society's apparent indifference to the "world beyond this one," spiritual pain is inescapable and widespread. Everyone needs a framework for meaning — a reason to live and a reason to die. People who are dying often seek a larger landscape of meaning and therefore need to feel part of a community that shares that meaning. In recent surveys, counseling on spiritual matters is rated among the top three necessities requested by the dying and their families.

These aspects of pain are all interrelated and sometimes hard to distinguish from one another. If efforts to manage pain focus on one aspect to the neglect of the others, the patient may not experience true relief of pain. Unrelieved pain can lead not only to depression and anger, but to asking for death for oneself or to obtaining it for others. As the Vatican *Declaration on Euthanasia*[14] notes, the pleas of the terminally ill who sometimes ask for death are not to be taken as a true desire for euthanasia or assisted suicide. Rather, they are more likely anguished pleas for effective relief of pain, for better medical care, for love.

MANAGING PAIN

Physical Pain

Physical pain is usually the easiest to control, yet standard American healthcare is still doing a poor job at managing it. While medical texts describe effective pharmacological and nonpharmacological approaches to controlling pain, most physical pain goes unrelieved. Some experts estimate that as many as 75 percent of patients in pain are inadequately treated, and 60 to 90 percent of those who are terminally ill experience severe to moderate pain sufficient to impair physical functioning, mood, and social interaction. Nearly 25 percent of cancer patients die with severe, unrelieved pain. How can we account for these sad statistics?

From the perspective of the patient, the thresholds of pain vary. Pain can increase out of fear, isolation, insomnia, or depression. Patients' responses to the treatment of pain also vary. One of the great problems patients have is finding an adequate language for expressing their pain so that it can be accurately identified and addressed. Some patients are reluctant to say anything at all about their pain because they feel others may judge them as weak, as wimps, as complainers, or as clock-watchers waiting for the next dose. Another problem of managing pain from the patient's perspective is that some choose not to comply with the therapeutic program, perhaps in order to avoid side effects of treatment which would impair attending to unfinished business, or perhaps simply as a way to assert some control in the face of losing control. Others may deny their pain in order to retain a feeling that they are still in control, despite evidence to the contrary. Still others may use their pain to shield themselves from more unwelcome issues. Others embrace pain believing that it has some redemptive value which they can offer to God.

While medical texts describe effective pharmacological and nonpharmacological approaches to controlling pain, most physical pain goes unrelieved.

Physicians also contribute to the failure to give patients relief from pain. Some are ignorant of the nature of pain. Others do not accurately diagnose the source of pain in the first place, or they fail to assess the patient at regular intervals to detect new pain-causing processes which may demand new therapies. Some simply do not believe the patient's description of pain. Still others do not try alternatives to drug therapy, such as electrical nerve stimulation, nerve blocks, biofeedback, deep massage, or non-Western modes, such as acupuncture and acupressure.

Some of those who use drug therapies are too timid in prescribing narcotics or neglect the appropriate use of aspirin-like drugs for the relief of bone pain. Narcotics may be underprescribed because of: (1) basic ignorance of the magnitude of the doses needed to combat severe pain; (2) inappropriate fear of causing respiratory distress; (3) misplaced anxiety about the hazards of addiction; (4) an irrational fear of civil or criminal prosecution; or (5) an overestimation of the side effects of some analgesics, such as potential addiction. Recent statistics estimate that over 90 percent of pain can be relieved, and usually by means of drugs. The challenge to physicians is to identify accurately the need for managing pain and then to use state-of-the-art techniques to control it.

An understanding of the current clinical art of managing pain will help caregivers to appreciate the possibilities within their reach. Healthcare professionals who are accustomed to giving one to two milligrams of morphine in the emergency room or coronary care unit for the relief of moderate acute pain need to know that some patients may need, and can tolerate, 1,000 milligrams or more of morphine per hour, as in intravenous infusion, to control the ferocious pain of some cancers. Such doses are not reached overnight but infusions are judiciously titrated upwards in measured increments until pain is contained. In this way respiratory distress does not occur, since unrelieved pain acts as a physiological antagonist to the respiratory depressant effect of the opiate drug.

Patients who are dying will eventually stop breathing whether they receive opiates or not. Unrelieved agony will shorten a life more surely than adequate doses of morphine. As a treatment for relieving genuine pain, opiate usage does not lead to addiction.

Yet, we are still far from the successful management of pain. To achieve the goal of successfully managing pain as a major dimension of compassionate care for the dying, we need to accomplish certain tasks:

1. Hospitals need to formulate policies for the acceptable use of narcotics to treat dying patients; they must not restrict opiate use but sanction it in necessary dosages to control pain without regard to vital signs.

2. Local experts need to be trained in the various methods for controlling pain by means of all available modalities — drugs, electrical stimulation, biofeedback, etc.

3. Medical students also need to be trained in the various methods for managing pain.

4. Pharmaceutical companies need to educate qualified professionals on the proper use of pain medications.

5. State-wide consultation networks for managing pain need to be developed.

6. Clinicians need to engage in dialogue with local medical associations, legislators, district attorneys, and others in order to assure their understanding of the appropriate use of opiates and to prevent ill-conceived policies or sanctions that may discourage the appropriate management of pain.

Psycho-Social-Spiritual Pain

The pain experienced in terminal illness is more than physical. It affects not only the patient's concept of self, but also his or her whole sense of being connected to others and to the world. The psycho-social-spiritual pain can: (1) overwhelm the dying patient's sense of being in control; (2) threaten the patient's sense of purpose or meaning; and (3) easily weaken the sense of being connected to others, since dying intensifies isolation by disrupting the patient's ordinary ways of making contact with others. Since our usual coping mechanisms are weakened or overwhelmed by the distress of dying, patients who are terminally ill are often left with feelings of powerlessness, hopelessness, and isolation. Any adequate plan for managing the psycho-social-spiritual pain, then, will have to address these conditions.

The Need for Emotional Support

Perhaps the most healing remedy to address the psycho-social-spiritual pain is the quality of the relationships sustained between the patient and the caregivers, and between the patient and his or her family. The healing quality of the therapeutic relationship can easily be weakened or threatened when emotional reactions experienced by patients, families, or caregivers are not adequately addressed. Some of the common emotional reactions include denial, anger, guilt, and fear.

◆ Denial is an early, strong emotion everyone experiences, when we knowingly or unknowingly try to give a situation the semblance that all is well. It is a natural built-in defense mechanism that helps the patient and caregivers select or reject a range of reactions, such as refusing to admit that the terminal diagnosis may be correct or refusing to admit that one has fear for self, for the future, or for one's ability to cope with dying. But denial is not always bad, and one does not always have to overcome it. Selective attention — dealing with a little of the truth and the feelings at a time — can be a way of coping with and alleviating the pain. Caregivers can, therefore, help patients by tolerating their denial and by not forcing the truth upon them. Ideally, families and caregivers will themselves not hide behind denial, which tends to isolate them from the patient. Rather, by facing the patient's impending death, they may allow the patient to cope with dying in the way that is tolerable for him or her.

◆ Patients are often angry at themselves for being sick. They also get angry at families and caregivers for their patronizing and overprotective behavior which seems to take away whatever sense of control, privacy, and independence patients may have left. Family members get angry for not being able to do more. Caregivers are angry for not being able to give definitive answers, clearer directions, or a cure. Everyone gets angry at everyone else for making unreasonable demands or for being so intrusive; or they are angry simply out of the frustration of feeling powerless and being trapped in a hopeless situation.

◆ Guilt may be provoked by feelings of anger, disgust, or contempt for someone we love. Patients feel guilty for being a burden on their family, or for not making amends for a broken relationship. Family members often feel guilty because they are not able to do enough for the patient, or because they did not identify the problem early enough, or did not seek help or get involved sooner. Caregivers may feel guilty for not being able to cure, relieve pain, or prolong life with better quality.

◆ Fears are many. The patient fears pain, isolation, losing control, and becoming dependent. Patients also fear what will happen to their loved ones (Will they run out of money? How will they get along?). They fear the unknown (How will I die? What will death be like?). They fear their own insignificance (Did my life mean anything to anyone? Does it mean anything now?). Families, too, fear the unknown. Caregivers fear mistakes and, sometimes, lawsuits.

The Need for Relatedness and Meaning

Emotions experienced by family members and caregivers may tempt them to ignore the dying person. Facing the fact that nothing more can be done to improve the medical condition of the dying patient and that death is imminent can often produce anxieties that cause people to withdraw from the patient. Sometimes anxiety is brought on because family members and caregivers cannot deal with their own feelings about death.

Everyone needs to be able to acknowledge these feelings and to realize that the dying need company and comfort more than treatment. When nothing more can be done to bring about a cure, we should cease doing what was once called for and intensify doing what is called for now. We must attend and keep company with the dying, try to make them comfortable, and treat them with as much dignity as possible.

Caregivers need to develop the skills that will enable them to support one another and to create a comfortable environment where patients meet death in a dignified way. The identity of the healthcare profession has been based on person-to-person healing. Because of the physician's central role in the healing relationship, the physician is in a strategic position to meet the patient's needs for feeling connected and finding meaning in the process of dying. But all the caregivers, not just the physician, play an important role in this matter. The feeling of being connected is at the heart of relieving the patient's social pain. When the patient experiences connectedness with the caregivers and feels heard and understood, the feeling of being socially isolated can be relieved. The caregivers' willingness to listen and to acknowledge the patient's pain gives him or her a feeling of worth, esteem, integrity, and wholeness. Life, even failing life, is bearable when sustained by the loving attention of others, even one other.

The family's connection to the patient is also important in

relieving social pain. While family relationships are subject to severe stress when a family member is dying, emotional reactions to the dying person can make it even more difficult for the patient to communicate his or her needs. Family dynamics and history can further complicate the relationship. Sometimes, as the patient becomes more dependent on others and a greater burden to them, those who have had a special place in his or her life become objects of worry. The dying patient may then feel as if he or she is failing to sustain the bonds of affection which bring a sense of worth and esteem. These emotions can lead the patient to a sense of loneliness which makes his or her fragile life no longer a gift sustained by the love of others but a burden no one wants to bear.

Life, even failing life, is bearable when sustained by the loving attention of others, even one other.

Feeling connected also enhances the patient's sense of meaning and purpose. The seeming meaninglessness of the boring round of daily routines and superficial relationships in the patient's life day after day provides no satisfying reason to live. When patients no longer see themselves as playing any significant part in the scheme of things, as a receiver or a contributor, then their courage and strength to participate in life weakens.

Pastoral care services can help to connect the patient to a larger framework of meaning by drawing upon his or her spiritual connections through the use of religious stories, rites, and symbols. These are valuable resources in the clinical setting for relieving the spiritual pain which inevitably comes to the terminally ill, who ask questions of meaning and of the place of God in their living and dying.

The Need for Truthful Communication

Truthful communication is at the heart of the therapeutic relationship. It is no wonder that defective communication (no information, deceptive information, or true information poorly communicated) is often at the root of medical malpractice suits. In the past, withholding information and the "therapeutic lie" were thought to be justified so as not to harm the patient by creating more distress through bad news. Today we realize that deception (stating what is untrue, omitting what is true, or telling what is true but in unintelligible language) undermines the trust which holds the healing relationship together. So, the real question for the physician is not "Should I tell the truth?" Rather, it is "How do I tell the truth in a way that will benefit the patient?"

The patient's comfort can be profoundly affected by the way the physician conveys information. Truthful communication stands between the extremes of benevolent deception and confronting the patient at point-blank range so as to destroy all hope. The need for truthful communication demands that the physician disclose information in a way, at a time, and in whatever increments necessary to allow the patient to assimilate and use the information. Grim news demands an especially tactful manner of telling so as to relieve suffering and to inspire courage and hope. In short, tact, timing, and style are as important as accuracy in a therapeutic conversation. Also, since the patient's condition changes and his or her ability to absorb information changes, an honest and open conversation must be ongoing.

In the course of this conversation, the following considerations may be helpful:

1. Good communication begins with good self-understanding and self-acceptance. We may easily project our own fears and uncertainties onto others when we are not able to recognize and acknowledge them in ourselves. We betray ourselves most conspicuously in nonverbal ways. Caregivers must be mindful, then, of their nonverbal signals: physical tension, nervous gestures, or the failure to make eye contact communicate more about one's own fears than they communicate about information pertinent to the patient. Caregivers must strive to understand what makes them uncomfortable with their task of communicating bad news. Is it due to anxiety about their own mortality? Is it a reluctance to admit failure? Is it a lack of communication skills? Is it a fear of adding to the patient's pain? Only when the caregiver has better self-understanding and self-acceptance will the therapeutic relationship truly be healing for the patient.

2. Caregivers must take time to talk *with* dying patients, not *at* them. Talking with patients about what is important to them or just sitting with them attentively in silence are both ways for caregivers to honor the dignity and experience of the patient and to serve as agents of healing. Active listening that tries to appreciate the reality of the patient's situation and that pays attention to the patient's concerns (important relationships, personal successes and anxieties, business interests, spiritual needs, superstitions, fantasies, questions, dreams, and hopes) creates a climate of openness for an easy exchange of ideas and feelings.

3. While patients with unmistakable symptoms usually already know their condition and are rarely surprised by grim news, most other patients want to know about their prognosis. Thus, health-care professionals should presume disclosing all available information unless the patient specifically wishes not to know. In that case, someone in the family ought to be told. But deceiving a patient, even when done for the patient's "good," only causes anxiety and threatens to undermine the trust that is necessary to make a therapeutic relationship effective. Shielding patients from unpleasant information is ultimately impossible; therefore, deception in any form, either by lying or by withholding informa-

tion, fuels an irretrievable sense of betrayal and prevents patients from trusting fully again.

4. Truthful communication tells patients no more than what is known about their condition or prognosis. Caregivers who admit their ignorance and describe the patient's condition or prognosis in a matter-of-fact manner, without making any false promises or flooding the patient with pity and sympathy, actually promote confidence. Patients who are assured that good care will be provided, that they are not being deceived, and that they will not be abandoned, will be better prepared to absorb the hard news and live with the uncertainties.

5. Caregivers should keep the patient as much in the driver's seat as possible by keeping the patient fully informed. Familiarity with the unpleasant facts of a terminal illness need not destroy hope or breed despair. Rather, patients who have access to the facts of their situation know what to expect and can feel more in control by reducing the chance of being surprised. The feeling of hopelessness quickly overwhelms those who have no say in determining the course of their own lives or have no opportunity to shape the events in which they participate. Those who feel more like victims than agents soon ask "Why struggle to survive?"

This brief review of pain and the managing of pain shows that caregivers must be able to adapt their methods and resources to the many dimensions of pain and to the diversity of their patients. Each patient experiences pain differently and to different degrees. Caregivers must try to understand each patient's pain in order to formulate an appropriate, individualized response. Comprehensive pain management will include not only specialized clinical programs to control physical pain, but also counseling and human support to minimize psychological pain, community support groups to counter social pain, and pastoral care resources to address spiritual pain.

Caregivers should keep the patient as much in the driver's seat as possible by keeping the patient fully informed.

INSTITUTIONAL RESPONSES

Healthcare institutions can organize themselves internally to offer optimal support for those who are dying and for their caregivers. A few suggestions are described here.

Integrated Treatment Plans

A lack of coordination of care can easily result when a patient is cared for by a number of specialists but no primary caregiver or attending physician takes a personal, overall responsibility. When the terminally ill patient and his or her family are receiving information from a variety of sources — often piecemeal and incomplete — all will experience a sense of fragmentation, a lack of appropriate and adequate information, and the absence of clear and holistic goals in the overall care of the patient.

For reasons such as these, the collaborative team model is the most effective approach for responding to the diverse aspects of pain in the dying person. This involves a team of healthcare professionals in which the primary caregiver coordinates the care plan and communicates with the patient, with family or surrogates, and with other professionals. All participants, especially the patient, are treated as active decision makers in implementing the care plan. Special effort is made to recognize emotional reactions and their meanings and to make appropriate referrals for professional assistance when necessary. Collaboration also includes sharing resources within the organization and outside it in order to assure continuity of care and the appropriate placement of the terminally ill patient upon discharge from the healthcare facility.

Hospitable Environment

The environment in which care is delivered is an important factor in the overall care of the patient, particularly when the patient dies in the institution. To provide the sense of dignity that a dying patient deserves, the healthcare facility should create a physical atmosphere that avoids these typical situations: (1) the surroundings generally lack aesthetic quality and are noisy; (2) patients often lack privacy, even in a "private" room; and (3) drab colors, no pictures, offensive odors, incessant beeps from machines and announcements over the P.A. system all contribute to an environment that is unpleasant, unattractive, and overstimulating to the senses of hearing and smelling. Since the dying person has few pleasures left, an environment that overloads the senses in such offensive ways offers little relief or satisfaction.

Institutional Policies

Good policies on advance directives and collaborative decision making can enhance the autonomy of the dying patient and clarify the roles and responsibilities of others involved in making decisions at the final stages of life. Such policies can alleviate physicians' fears of legal liability; and, at the same time, they may foster care which enables the dying to live their last days in as peaceful and uncomplicated a fashion as possible.

Institutional Ethics Committees

The institutional ethics committee can be a valuable resource in making difficult ethical decisions. A forum for ethical reflection, dialogue, and planning, this multidisciplinary group of people serves the institution by promoting education, assisting in the development of policies, and functioning as a resource for consultation in difficult situations. While the primary purpose of the ethics committee is to advise the institution and to promote the well-being of the patients, it offers an added benefit as a forum for the resolution of difficult cases thereby avoiding recourse to the courts for settling conflicts.

Educating the Public

Developments in medicine, especially advances in the use of technology, drug therapies, and surgery, have captured the interest of the public. Recent court rulings have added to the growing concern about the use of these medical advances to prolong life. Discussions on healthcare reform in America have also made more people conscious of their responsibility to take care of their health. More people want to learn about good health habits and about expert opinion on the proper use of advanced technologies to sustain life. Healthcare institutions, in cooperation with schools and parishes, can now make a significant contribution to preventive medicine by sponsoring more educational programs. The time is ripe for coordinated education of the public.

Hospice

A comprehensive philosophy of care for people in the final phases of a terminal illness, hospice affirms life and regards dying as a normal process. Hospice emphasizes controlling pain and symptoms in order to enhance the quality of life rather than to attempt to cure an illness or to extend life. The purpose of hospice is to allow patients and their families to live each day as fully and comfortably as possible and to assist in dealing with the stress caused by illness, death, and grief. Hospice uses a team approach to focus on the physical, emotional, spiritual, and social needs of patients and their families. The interdisciplinary team consists of physicians, nurses, aides, social workers, trained volunteers, and pastoral counselors who work together to provide coordination and continuity of patient/family care, and also offer follow-up services for the family and grief counseling after the patient has died.

> Managing pain effectively requires a comprehensive program such as that exemplified in the hospice philosophy of care.

The modern hospice movement began in 1967 when Dr. Cecily Saunders opened the now famous St. Christopher's Hospice in London. The hospice movement emerged in America in 1974 in New Haven, CT, and has grown to nearly 2,000 programs today. Yet, it is still not a well-known or often utilized program, partially because of the social stigma related to death and the common public and professional perception that hospice signifies failure or giving up. Adequate reimbursement for hospice services is another public concern and is currently being addressed through legislatures and third-party payers. Improved education of healthcare professionals, the religious community, and the general public about the availability, appropriate referral, and correct utilization of hospice services is necessary to improve awareness and to ensure quality care for the dying and their families.

Conclusion

Appropriate care of the dying in the clinical setting seeks to respect the integrity of the patient as a person through the final days of life. Thus, appropriate clinical care tries to guarantee at least the following:

1. That the patient will be kept as free of pain as possible so that he or she may die comfortably and with dignity
2. That the patient will receive continuity of care and not be abandoned or lose personal identity
3. That the patient will retain as much control as possible over decisions regarding his or her care and will be allowed to refuse whatever further life-prolonging technological interventions are offered
4. That the patient will be heard as an individual with personal fears, thoughts, feelings, values, and hopes
5. That the patient will be able to die where he or she wants to die.

Implications for Catholic Healthcare

◆ Physical pain is not effectively managed for a significant percentage (75 percent or more) of patients. What are we doing to become more knowledgeable about the nature of pain and about using state-of-the-art techniques to manage it?

◆ Since pain in its multiple dimensions often accompanies terminal illness, what comprehensive programs do we have for managing all dimensions of pain, focusing not on one aspect to the neglect of others?

◆ Knowing that pain is more than physical and includes psychosocial-spiritual aspects, what specific steps are we taking to support positive relationships between patients and caregivers, between patients and their families, and between patients and their religious beliefs and practices in order to satisfy the needs for emotional support, for feeling connected, and for meaning?

◆ Truthful communication is at the heart of the therapeutic relationship. How do our programs for professional caregivers foster an adequate self-understanding and self-acceptance so that we can present information on terminal illness in a way, at a time, and in whatever increments necessary to allow patients to assimilate and use the information which belongs to them?

◆ Managing pain effectively requires a comprehensive program such as that exemplified in the hospice philosophy of care. What have we learned from hospice, or in what ways have we adopted the hospice concept so that care will be coordinated in a collaborative manner, so that dying patients will live in a supportive environment, and so that institutional policies and practices will promote their well-being?

PART IV

THEOLOGICAL, MORAL, AND PASTORAL RESPONSE

This section will consider the experience of suffering and dying in the light of faith. We aspire to be able to give meaning to what seems so meaningless and to find a way to respond that will express our faith and be filled with love and hope.

DEATH AS EVENT

Death is the end of life as we know it. While death terminates our days on earth, it also completes our life and our contribution to God's creation.

While everyone can easily recognize the distressing prospect that death is the termination of earthly life, it takes a different perspective to see that death completes life. Dr. Elisabeth Kübler-Ross, for example, describes death as "the final stage of growth." Her life's work with the dying helped to shape this special perspective. The beauty, rather than the shock, of her message reminds us that we have only one life to live, and it challenges us to live life to the fullest right up to the end. Also, it helps us to appreciate that death is not simply something that happens to us from the outside. While we do not want to deny the passive dimension of death, since our bodies do break down and there is nothing we can do to stop that, we must remember that death is also the final act of living, generated from within the person, bringing to fulfillment all that is valuable to that person. In death we can sum up all that we have been in life and bring that into the presence of God where life is changed, not ended.

"Gaudium et Spes,"[15] a document issued by the Second Vatican Council, underscored the Catholic conviction that God has called us to an endless sharing of divine life beyond death (no. 18). We proclaim this mystery of faith in our Eucharistic acclamation: "Dying you destroyed our death, rising you restored our life. Lord Jesus, come in glory." The death/resurrection of Jesus has freed us from death. Another Eucharistic acclamation affirms this mystery of faith as well: "Lord, by your cross and resurrection you have set us free. You are the Savior of the world." Such a conviction of faith arouses hope that through death we find true life with God ("Gaudium et Spes,"[16] no. 18).

But even for believers, letting go of earthly existence is difficult. We rightly fear death because we lose so much in dying. We lose people we love, we lose our work, and we lose all those things which have given us gladness in life as we have known it. Further, we are bothered by the prospect that our lives will be forgotten. Or, as Leo Tolstoy wrote so eloquently in *The Death of Ivan Illich*, we fear the final realization that we have not really lived the lives we most deeply wanted to live. As "Gaudium et Spes"[17] pointed out, we do not want the total disappearance that death brings. Yet all our turning to technology to keep death at bay cannot calm our anxiety over death. The desire to live is inescapably lodged in our hearts. We cannot ultimately control or avoid death from happening to us (no. 18). Therefore, we also fear death because it opens a door to the unknown.

Given the ambiguity and threat which death poses, it is not surprising that people avoid thinking and talking about death, deny its imminence in the face of medical diagnosis, and take heroic measures to prevent death at all costs and to postpone it for as long as possible.

As members of the Christian faith, we must take these fears seriously and stand with people in their anxiety in order to share effectively the perspective that can transform suffering and death from a mere termination to a completion of life.

TRANSFORMATION THROUGH SUFFERING AND DYING

Our first reaction to suffering and dying is to resist it. We direct all our skills, medications, and treatments against illness and against premature death. The great advances medical science has made in recent decades reminds us of the fierceness with which it has struggled against illness and death. More people in our society are able to live longer and with a better quality of life because of what medical science has achieved in its unrelenting fight to rehabilitate injuries and to cure sickness.

Suffering

Pain and suffering are closely related, but they are not the same. While we know that physical pain remains the major cause of suffering, and while we must continue to do what we can to find more effective means to relieve it, we also know that not everyone with pain is also suffering. Suffering is a personal matter, which is as much a function of an individual's attitude as it is of physical causes. For example, two people may have the same physical condition, but only one of them may be suffering with it.

We experience suffering as a state of distress when we sense that our physical condition may harm or destroy us. The presence and extent of suffering, though, can only be known to the sufferer. We have no objective way to measure or to verify the claims of patients that their suffering is unbearable. So, if we want to know whether someone in pain is also suffering, we have to ask them.

People in pain report suffering when they feel out of control. The dying person is at the mercy of the medical world which is filled with procedures, technologies, and a language which can be confusing, unintelligible, and oppressive. All the efforts designed to set the patient free can actually oppress and hold the patient captive. When this happens, patients report that they are suffering. People in pain also suffer when pain cannot be relieved, when its source is unknown, when it becomes overwhelming or seems endless, or when the person can find no meaning in it.

It is no wonder then that the ever-present question in the minds and hearts, and often on the lips, of those suffering from pain is "Why?" It is a question not only about the source of pain or cause of suffering ("What have I done to deserve this?" "Why me?" "Why do bad things happen to good people?"), but more importantly it is a question of meaning and purpose ("What's life all about?"). In a culture that cannot depend on religious insights into suffering to address the deeper questions, all kinds of interventions, even euthanasia and assisted suicide, may seem to be inevitable.

In a culture that cannot depend on religious insights into suffering to address the deeper questions, all kinds of interventions, even euthanasia and assisted suicide, may seem to be inevitable.

Meaning in Suffering

We turn, then, to our tradition of faith to find meaning in the mysteries of suffering and death. The Catholic tradition teaches that suffering can be transformed. The Rite for the Pastoral Care of the Sick observes: "Christians feel and experience pain as do all other people; yet their faith helps them to grasp more deeply the mystery of suffering and to bear their pain with greater courage. From Christ's words they know that sickness has meaning and value for their own salvation and for the salvation of the world" (Introduction, no. 1).

Suffering offers the Christian the chance to identify with the suffering of Christ. This "function" of suffering is its glorification and its relief. If, through suffering, the sufferer is brought nearer to the cherished goal of a closer bonding with God in Christ, then that person may have no sense of suffering because of the comfort of the spiritual experience it offers. The bonding with Christ is the means for relieving the suffering.

This conviction does not make a virtue out of pain or attribute any intrinsic value to suffering in itself. As Pope John Paul II observed in his apostolic letter, *The Christian Meaning of*

Suffering[18], "Suffering is, in itself, an experience of evil" (no. 26). Furthermore, the Rite for the Pastoral Care of the Sick points out: "Part of the plan laid out by God's providence is that we should fight strenuously against all sickness and carefully seek the blessings of good health, so that we may fulfill our role in human society and in the Church" (Introduction, no. 3). When this is not possible, however, the power of faith permits us to find meaning in the experiences of suffering and dying and thereby transform them.

Both the terminally ill and their caregivers can see through the eyes of faith that there is power in our deterioration, freedom in our dependency, hope in what appears to be defeat, and life on the other side of death. This vision does not come automatically. It often entails a struggle with periods of doubt and feelings of anger, loss, or abandonment. But with the help of compassionate caregivers and the support of a community of faith, the dying are able to understand these paradoxes and draw upon that capacity of their human spirit to "feel whole" in the midst of pain, frailty, and deterioration.

The foundations for finding meaning in suffering lie in the very dignity of the human person, which is established in creation. Our faith proclaims that God created all things to be good. At the climax of creation, God fashioned humanity in the divine image. God declared us to be "very good" (Gn 1:31). As bearers of God's image, we have a dignity which is never lost, even when we are diminished or disfigured by pain and suffering.

The dignity of the human person is deepened through the mystery of the Incarnation. Every aspect of human existence is transformed by its direct and redemptive relationship with Jesus the Christ, the one in whom God took on a human form and entered fully into human life. Joined with the Risen One in baptism, we are now "temples of the Holy Spirit," "temples of the living God" (1 Cor 3:17, 6:19; 2 Cor 6:16). God's Holy Spirit dwells in us, infusing our lives and our suffering with grace and holiness.

The Transformation of Suffering

The true depth of the meaning of the Incarnation and God's ultimate loving embrace of humanity is revealed in the cross. Through Jesus, God not only entered into human life, but God also entered into human suffering and death. Jesus did not court suffering for its own sake, but neither did he deny it. Jesus experienced what all human beings dread, death. The passion of Christ reminds us that there is no misery, no fear, no sorrow which is not somehow held in the heart of the one who has chosen to share our existence with us. As Pope John Paul II affirmed in his letter, *The Christian Meaning of Human Suffering*[19]: "One can say that with the passion of Christ all human suffering has found itself in a new situation . . . In the cross of Christ not only is the Redemption accomplished through suffering, but also human suffering itself has been redeemed" (no. 19).

The ministry of Jesus tells us that God reaches into life to heal and to show mercy. The crucified Jesus tells us that God goes with us all the way through suffering even into death. But there is still more. The story does not end with death. Death does not have the last word, life does. The story of the life/death/resurrection of Jesus tells us that the tragedy of suffering and dying is transformed: "But in fact Christ has been raised from the dead" (1 Cor 15:20). The resurrection of Jesus teaches us that God is stronger than death, that God gives life, creates, lures us into intimacy, and makes us live. Suffering and death cannot — and will not — be stronger than the love of God. God's love, revealed in Jesus, gives us the strength to hope for the fullness of life in God's kingdom, where we will find the dissolution of all suffering and the enjoyment of unimpeded dignity for all persons.

Suffering and death remind us that God's reign is not yet fully present. Creation, the incarnation of Jesus, his suffering/death/resurrection all remind us, however, that we are sacred and intensely loved. Through these mysteries God promises that we shall know a life that triumphs over death, a love that conquers death. These mysteries tell us, as well, that the terrible isolation of suffering and death is not final. The Risen One, surrounded by all the saints, goes with us, accompanies us into death, and invites us to participate in resurrection.

Suffering and death cannot — and will not — be stronger than the love of God.

Faith allows us to overcome suffering through our love of and hope in God whose love for us vanquishes the sorrow of the grave. By seeing God's response to human suffering through Christ's love, and by sharing the mystery of his cross and resurrection already affirmed by legions of holy ones, a dying person is enabled to overcome the sense of suffering's uselessness. Isolation and victimization can yield to peace and courage. "O death, where is your victory? O death, where is your sting?" (1 Cor 15:55).

Based on the power of divine love to transform suffering and death from absolute evils to personal triumphs, the moral principles which the Catholic Church upholds can provide a hopeful perspective for the healthcare professionals who direct the care of the dying.

MORAL AND PASTORAL PRINCIPLES

The Vatican *Declaration on Euthanasia*[20] draws upon the three principles which are the pillars supporting the Roman Catholic teaching on conserving health and life — sanctity of life, God's dominion and human stewardship, and the prohibition against killing.

Sanctity of Life

The principle of sanctity of life states that each person is of incalculable worth and has inherent dignity because he or she is made in the image of God, redeemed by Christ, and called to share fully in the life of the triune God. The inherent dignity of human life entitles each person to the same basic right to life and pastoral care regardless of age or condition. The value and dignity of human life are guaranteed because they result solely from God's creating and sustaining us by love, not because of our having had personal achievements or having been useful to others.

The proper respect for the sanctity of life lies between two extremes. One extreme is "physical vitalism," which advocates the absolute value of maintaining biological life regardless of other values, such as independence, loss of dignity, preventing pain, or saving resources. Physical vitalism can lead to the abuse of overtreatment, that is, doing everything possible to prolong physical life while believing that no cost is too great and no chance too remote to save life.

The other extreme is "utilitarian pessimism" which values life for its social usefulness, and advocates ending life when it becomes frustrating, useless, or burdensome. Thus, only the strongest and fittest are to have access to treatment. This extreme can lead to the abuse of undertreatment, especially for the disabled, for it focuses on their lack of qualities that enable them to realize full human potential and/or to be of some benefit to others.

Between these two extremes, the Catholic principle of sanctity of life affirms that life is a basic good, but not an absolute one to be preserved at all costs. Physical life is a basic good because it is fundamental for achieving all other values, and it sets the limits for promoting human well-being.

Two obligations flow from the sanctity of life principle: (1) the obligation to nurture and support life, and (2) the obligation not to harm or destroy life. Therefore, the sanctity of life principle gives a strong presumption in favor of sustaining life. Anyone who would take life or fail to prevent death must have a very serious resolve to warrant overriding the presumption.

Often, the pastoral caregiver is in the most advantageous position to encourage the patient and family members to honor these obligations. Finding the balance between extremes and affirming the sanctity of life while coping with intense emotion are exceedingly difficult. A skilled caregiver who shares the experience with the patient, the family, and medical experts can offer both the perspective and the support needed to make appropriate decisions.

God's Dominion and Human Stewardship

The principle of God's dominion and human stewardship acknowledges that we are creatures who owe our creation to God. Human life is God's gift to us, and our responsibility to God is to cherish it as a sacred trust. We have only a right to the *use* of human life, not to dominion over it. Human responsibility for life is one of stewardship, not ownership. No one can claim total mastery over one's own or another's life. Absolute dominion is an exclusively divine prerogative. Yet our human glory is that we are not fated to be mere victims of biological forces, since we exercise responsible stewardship of our lives by going beyond our physical limitations as well as consenting to them.

We can go beyond some of the physical limits of our nature by cooperating with God who continues to open new spiritual possibilities for human well-being. A pastoral caregiver, attentive to the movement of God in a patient's life, can help the person recognize these new possibilities. One of the greatest of these pastoral services is to help people see their bodily condition in the context of their whole life and spiritual beliefs. The patient's suffering may then seem less burdensome and he or she can even regain a sense of being a contributor, either by "filling up what is lacking in Christ's sufferings" or by being "a witness to others of the essential or higher things" (Rite, no. 3).

By placing importance on spiritual understanding, we also encourage patients to make reasonable efforts to maintain life and to restore health. When patients avail themselves of treatments which they appreciate as a benefit, then they can live with hope that sees every moment, even moments of pain, fear, despair, or struggle, as occasions for growth. But life and hope have reasonable limits to which each person must consent. Just as one must not sacrifice life as long as there is reasonable hope for its well-being, one also must not sacrifice hope when life has reached its reasonable limits. When the dying patient can no longer appreciate treatments as a benefit, and creative living becomes impossible, then hope should focus on the eternal life after death.

Human responsibility for life is one of stewardship, not ownership.

No one should be expected to sustain this hope alone. The Church's pastoral care of the sick is particularly responsive to those at this stage of an illness. Through prayer, sacraments, community presence, and physical care, the Church accompanies a seriously ill or dying person by exercising joint stewardship with that person for the life that belongs to God.

The Prohibition Against Killing

The third principle is the prohibition against killing, which entails the obligation to protect life and the obligation not to destroy or injure human life directly, especially the life of the innocent and vulnerable.

To clarify this principle, it is necessary to examine the distinction between killing and allowing to die. Killing is any intentional action or omission bringing about the death of another; the cause of death is the human intervention or omission. Allowing to die is withholding or withdrawing futile or overly burdensome treatment; therefore, the disease or fatal condition overtaking the person is the cause of death. Catholic teaching asserts that allowing a person to die by omitting useless and/or burdensome treatment is permissible and morally different from killing. This teaching has been expressed through the distinction between ordinary and extraordinary treatment — a distinction that has been practically synonymous with the Catholic medical-moral tradition on the prolongation of life.

But the familiar terms "ordinary" and "extraordinary" can be very misleading when explaining the substance of this teaching. For example, the terms easily obscure *where* we focus our attention in a clinical judgment and *on whom* we focus it. The Vatican *Declaration on Euthanasia* has recognized the ambiguity of these terms and suggests that we might more effectively refer to "proportionate" and "disproportionate" treatment. Such designation clarifies our focus and avoids the confusion between the medical and moral meanings of this distinction.

From the medical point of view, the distinction is relative to the present state of medical science. This makes "ordinary" treatment whatever is standard practice with respect to the particular disease or condition. "Extraordinary" treatment would be whatever is considered novel or experimental. According to the medical understanding of this distinction, we can make a list of the treatments that are/were ordinary and extraordinary at any particular time in the development of medicine.

We could not make such a list from a moral point of view. The moral focus is *not* on the category of disease, the state of medical science, the type of treatment itself, or whether the treatment is simple, customary, noninvasive, or inexpensive. Rather, the true ethical considerations focus on the proportion between the benefit the patient would be able to appreciate from the treatment and the burden the patient would endure. For this reason, this principle is sometimes referred to as the burden/benefit principle.

To make proper use of this moral principle, we need to measure the proportionate benefits and burdens for each particular patient, and from the patient's perspective. The same person-centered approach governs pastoral care, determining what issues to bring up, how directly to deal with them, and what type of pastoral care this particular person needs at this time. Both pastoral care and the application of ethical principles are, therefore, "case specific."

In applying this principle, we must avoid generalities that say *all* patients of a certain class (such as persistent vegetative state, renal failure, Alzheimer's, and the like) need not be treated, or *all* treatments of a particular sort (medically dispensed fluids and nutrition, a respirator, dialysis, transplants) need not be used because they are always disproportionate. Rather, we must examine every treatment from the patient's perspective in order to determine whether it provides a benefit proportionate to the burden the patient will have to bear. If the reasonably foreseen benefits to that patient (such as cure, reduced pain, restored consciousness and bodily functions) outweigh the burdens to the patient or to others, then the treatment is morally obligatory.

If the reasonably foreseen benefits to that patient outweigh the burdens to the patient or to others, then the treatment is morally obligatory.

But the treatment is not obligatory if it would be disproportionately burdensome or futile. Some guidelines suggest that treatment is judged to be a burden if it: (1) produces excessive pain and suffering for the patient; (2) is repugnant; (3) impairs bodily functioning; (4) suppresses consciousness; (5) is too expensive for the patient, the family, or the community; (6) requires an investment in technology or personnel disproportionate to the results; or (7) requires inequitable allocation of social resources. A treatment is futile when it offers no probable hope of success to restore the patient to a state of reasonable well-being.

Moreover, the burden/benefit principle makes no moral distinction between withholding or withdrawing life-sustaining treatment (whether it be a mechanical respirator, a cardiac pacemaker, a renal dialysis machine, antibiotics, or medically dispensed nutrition and hydration) when its use is futile or would produce burdens disproportionate to the benefits the patient could appreciate. In these futile cases of underlying total pathology, there is no question of murder, suicide, or assisted suicide, since the physical cause of death is ultimately the fatal disease or condition which required the use of such treatment in the first place. All those involved, caregivers and patient, should humbly accept the inherent limitations of the human condition. When this moment arrives, it is also time to begin celebrating the life which is coming to its completion, either through the formal rituals of the Church or through spontaneous and cultural expressions appropriate to the dying person.

Related to this discussion is the use of narcotics with the specific intention of relieving pain, even if it is foreseen that their use will shorten life. While some people may find the experience of pain to be a moment of spiritual growth, self-discovery, or conversion, others find that pain victimizes, diminishes, and destroys their dignity. The Catholic tradition does not require people to suffer with pain. We can reasonably presume that most people would want to be kept free of pain, even if they do not explicitly say so. The effective use of narcotics to alleviate or to suppress pain is the prudent thing to do, even though they may eventually cause loss of consciousness or a quicker death. In all cases, the use of pain relief should be as much as possible under the control of the patient, who must decide what level of pain is tolerable and how much medication is beneficial.

While these principles have served the Catholic community well in meeting our moral responsibility to conserve life and promote health, they are not by themselves sufficient as a moral or pastoral response to the care of the suffering and dying. Moral and pastoral commitments are only partially expressed in principles. Action is also required. Moral virtues must be reflected in ethical behavior and in pastoral practice so that we may enact our Christian vision in the face of suffering and death.

MORAL VIRTUES AND PASTORAL PRACTICE

The moral character of our community embodies the truth expressed in our principles. What often makes our moral positions so unconvincing is not our principles or our logic in using them, but our ethical behavior which ultimately gives witness to our convictions. Paying attention to our character and our ethical practices is of grave importance in these days when euthanasia and assisted suicide are being promoted so aggressively. Whether the Catholic community will be able to influence public opinion on these issues depends a great deal on the kind of community we become.

In matters of morality, giving witness to our beliefs is more compelling than presenting arguments. Principles may teach, but shining examples bring principles to life and influence opinion more strongly. The true significance of our Catholic opposition to euthanasia and assisted suicide ultimately rests on the kind of ethical behavior we display, which reflects our convictions about God's sovereignty over life and the transformative meaning of suffering.

To carry on the mission of Jesus by responding to human suffering and death, healing communities must embody virtues that bear convincing witness in both a personal and a corporate manner regarding the care of the dying. What kind of community should we be to help people face the end of their lives with a sense of completion rather than hastening their termination through lethal intervention? Three characteristics of a virtuous community stand out: interdependence, care, and hospitality.

A Community of Interdependence

We have already seen that one of the major features of our society is individualism, which influences attitudes and practices toward the suffering and dying. Individualism isolates people into islands of self-interest and thereby blunts their sense of social responsibility for the common good. Also, it asserts that independence, not interdependence, is the key to human dignity.

The challenge to the Catholic community in the face of this cultural attitude is to care for the dying in a way that embodies the truth of interdependence. St. Paul's teachings maintain that all those united to Christ form one body and are members of one another; therefore, a one-sided emphasis on either independence or dependence is incorrect. Just as the body cannot be identified by just one of its parts, neither can any one part take the place of any other. Each contributes to the whole.

Catholic healthcare professionals must meet this challenge on two fronts, the personal and the corporate.

The Personal Front

On the personal front, we must examine the character of relationships in our healthcare institutions. One of the values at the foundation of the Catholic healthcare mission is the belief that the healing relationship is a mutually redemptive experience. It is as much a privilege to give as it is to receive. In healing, all give and all receive. The healing relationship is not to be a power play of the powerful and healthy oppressing the weak and sick. The commitment to healthcare embodies the general moral commitment to be partners with one another in an interdependent relationship sustained by trust and honesty.

> What kind of community should we be to help people face the end of their lives with a sense of completion rather than hastening their termination through lethal intervention?

1. Trust makes a therapeutic relationship possible. Patients trust that physicians will act in their best interests; and physicians trust that patients will accept their medical knowledge and skill as instruments that promote the patients' good. Trust easily conflicts with the desire to be autonomous and to exercise absolute control over everything. One of the ways to sustain trust is to keep confidences, for example. Keeping confidences enables partners to retain control over information which properly belongs to them. The need for trust in the healing relationship is a clear reminder that we do not have control over everything and that we are interdependent partners who need one another.

2. Honesty comes easily when trust is secure. The healing relationship is held together by honest exchange, occurring not just once, but over and over again. The therapeutic process is often impaired because of deceptions. Patients often put physicians in ethical binds because they fail to be honest in a number of ways.

For example, patients are dishonest when they do not comply with their prescribed plan of treatment, or when they fail to take preventive measures by developing unhealthy patterns of diet, work, and exercise. Patients, who ignore or deny warning symptoms from their bodies or hide symptoms by failing to express or not express clearly enough what they are experiencing and really want, are also being dishonest with their physicians.

Physicians, too, must exhibit honesty in a number of ways, not the least of which is in seeking informed consent. Honesty requires clear and timely communication of the diagnosis, prognosis, risks and benefits of possible treatments or nontreatments. This information should be discussed a little at a time, in a style which the patient can absorb. Poor communication on the part of physicians is one of the most common causes of malpractice suits. Honest communication from physicians can enable patients to participate in making decisions about their lives and in carrying out their part in the plan of treatment. Deception only undermines the trust which holds together the therapeutic relationship of interdependence.

The same values of trust and honesty govern pastoral care, not only between the caregiver and the patient but also between the caregiver and the medical staff. A pastoral caregiver should not get caught in the middle between the patient and the healthcare professional or appear to take sides if that relationship is not harmonious. On the other hand, the pastoral caregiver can mediate differences and communicate information so that mutual bonds are strengthened and better medical care is offered.

The Corporate Front

Corporately, pastoral caregivers and the Catholic healthcare community can give witness to the liberating and life-giving potential of interdependence by being catalysts for collaboration among other communities which have an interest in the care of the dying. The corporate network of hospitals, parishes, schools, and religious organizations can be drawn out of their isolation and integrated into a comprehensive program of healthcare. Pastoral care departments and mission effectiveness committees could lead this outreach effort and provide an example of interdependence by doing so.

The Paradigm of Curing

To be a community of care calls for a definite shift in the way we imagine the master plan for the practice of healthcare. Healthcare is governed, for the most part, by the paradigm of *curing*, propelled by a bias toward acute-care, high-technology medicine. The cultural context discussed in Part I emphasized that the massive presence of technology is a necessary fact in modern medicine. As the delivery of healthcare became more technologically resourceful, skilled technical intervention forced aside "human-touch" practices such as expressing concern for and keeping compassionate company with patients. Merely "caring" appears in the technological world of modern medicine as the consolation prize awarded when scientific knowledge and technical skills do not win.

For example, the paradigm of curing easily falls prey to the technological domination of modern medicine — if something can be done, it must be done. It also easily makes an idol of physical life and fuels the impulse to use medicine's power to prolong life, even under conditions one would personally find unacceptable. The idolatry of life takes form in the conviction that the inability to cure or to prevent death is a failure of modern medicine. The fallacy of this logic is that the healing responsibility ends when all curing treatments are exhausted.

In many ways, pastoral care has adopted the standard medical model, where curing and crisis intervention are the major goals. Conscious of inappropriate moralizing in the past and relying on therapeutic techniques borrowed from psychology, pastoral caregivers often have felt they were on the outer edges of the healing process and have been embarrassed about discussing spiritual issues or praying with patients. Where this has been the case, healthcare has been delivered on almost exclusively medical terms without integrating pastoral care into the overall plan of treatment. The goal of attending to the whole person has often been neglected.

The Paradigm of Caring

The increased public interest in euthanasia and assisted suicide draws our attention to the "curing" limits of medicine. We eventually wear out even if we do have access to a vast array of technical assistance. Healthcare, under the paradigm of *caring*, accepts decline and death as part of being human, since everyone suffers from a condition which cannot be "cured" — namely, being a mortal creature. Medicine cannot succeed in holding death at bay indefinitely. Death will ultimately come. When medical therapy can no longer attain its goals of preserving health or relieving suffering, and further treatment becomes futile or overly burdensome, then the moral obligation is to cease doing what is medically useless and to intensify efforts to ease the burden of dying. The paradigm of caring allows us to realistically face the limits of our mortality and of our medical power with an attitude that does not despair. In this paradigm, "caring" is not the consolation prize for a cure that could not be attained, but it is integral to the style and plan of treatment of the whole person.

The Virtues of a Community of Care

◆ Caring is the virtue which enables a person to enter another's life and through human empathy help make it more meaningful. In the case of the sick and dying, this might involve a cure but more often it means keeping company with a person during a difficult period of life. This kind of caring does not lend itself to quick fixes, even if the caregiver desires to solve someone's problem or to relieve someone's suffering.

True caring involves persistent presence, careful listening, and a willingness to enter deeply into another person's life in order to help carry the burden that person feels. The Catholic tradition highly values life as a basic condition necessary to achieve all other values. But our beliefs do not demand an idolatrous reverence which makes physical life an absolute value which must be sustained at all costs. A caring community can help a patient bear reasonable burdens which come as part of the limitations of being human. But when burdens become overwhelming, then the caring community can base its actions on the Catholic tradition that maintains that no one is morally obliged to bear burdens beyond one's capacity. Healthcare professionals and pastoral caregivers can help the patient to say, "Stop! Enough is enough."

◆ Courage is another virtue of a caring community, whose members "take heart" to stick through hard times, to take risks, to face darkness, to cope with tragedy. Courage empowers physicians to fulfill their covenant with society to act in the best interests of patients even when doing nothing is the only thing left to do. Courage is what everyone needs when the possibility of being restored to health is out of the question. In our Promethean society, which feeds on the myth that everything can be conquered, it takes courage for a person to face up to the reality that we all shall die. Courage is the willingness to face the truth about one's situation, to take the next step to change what can be changed, and then to accept what cannot be changed but only endured. A courageous community shares fears, fantasies, hopes, doubts, asks for and gives help, and bears one another's burdens. Courage enables us to let go so that new forms of life might rise from the darkness.

Courage also assumes proper responsibility for one's treatments. For example, many people fear being a victim of dependency, pain, and disability more than they fear death. The fear of being trapped in unacceptable conditions of dependency and disability brought about by medicine's power to prolong dying encourages the movement toward euthanasia. The request for euthanasia is asserted as a last gasp to avoid the excessive treatment which robs the dying person of a sense of self-direction and dignity. Unfortunately, the healthcare community will continue to find itself making many more difficult choices that it would like to avoid unless its consumers (patients) exercise personal courage to control the way they will live and die. If caregivers could encourage patients to set limits on their own treatments and properly inform them how they might do this, through ongoing conversation with their physician and family or even through the use of legal documents if needed, then euthanasia would not be necessary as a means of assuring their dignity and autonomy. It takes courage to educate people that technology cannot and will not replace compassionate love and caring. It also takes courage to accept that responding to the dying with compassionate love, and not with heroic technical measures, is an appropriate response to our mortality.

Healthcare accepts decline and death as part of being human, since everyone suffers from a condition which cannot be "cured" — namely, being a mortal creature.

◆ Perseverance is the virtue that stretches the boundaries of courage and each person to proclaim: "I'll get through this; I'll hang in there." A persevering community stays with a person as long as necessary and does not crumble when the going gets rough, but taps into the reservoirs of trust — in God, in one another, in one's self — to draw upon the strength of earlier times when confidence was high and self-esteem was secure. Perseverance makes possible doing and receiving the daily tasks of long-term care — activities such as eating, bathing, and toilet functions — without viewing them as demeaning. To do for others what they cannot do for themselves requires supportive emotional intimacy, commitment, time, and resources. Families sometimes pool their resources in order to persevere through long-term sufferings and finally the death of a loved one; and caregivers are often the privileged supporters and affirmers of this grace in action.

◆ Compassion is the companion of courage and perseverance. It responds to the reality of suffering with supportive emotional intimacy and hope. In a world where suffering is real, compassion means to suffer with another. It pushes the boundaries of care further by allowing persons with a special kind of courage to be present even in the remotest corners of another's suffering. In the cross of Jesus Christ, we see the reality and power of God suffering with us. Compassion reinforces the Christian conviction that suffering need not diminish the dignity of the human person but invites co-sufferers to share it and to transform it. The Christian pastoral response to those who suffer is to keep company with them, to relieve what distress we can, but above all to assure them that they do not suffer alone.

◆ Humility is necessary to deliver care without viewing any parts of it as demeaning, and humility is necessary to receive care and to accept being dependent on others for those things which one cannot do for oneself. While it may be more blessed to give than to receive, it is considerably more uncomfortable to receive than to give. Humility does not come easily, especially to Americans who pride themselves on their independence and their giving. Our dignity is assaulted by the progressive loss of bodily control, of physical energy, of social contacts, and by the passing glance of the young and healthy that tells us we are sick and dying. These situations humiliate us.

It bears remembering that humility, human, and earth all have the same word root — humus. God took the dust of the earth, breathed into it, and brought man and woman into being. We have been destined for humility ever since: "Remember, you are dust and unto dust you shall return." Humility should not be confused with submissive servility, self-diffidence, self-hate, or infantile docility. Humility means being down to earth about ourselves. It is the gracious acceptance of ourselves as creatures and acceptance of God as Creator. This may seem so obvious, yet it often takes illness or death to impress the idea on our minds. We are mortal, "vessels of clay" (2 Cor 4:7), fragile, and ultimately powerless. Only God is without limit and all-powerful.

Theologians have long noted that our faithfulness to God as the absolute sovereign is challenged by the temptation to participate in idolatry. In medicine, the high god in the pantheon of idols is technology. When medicine makes advances which conquer "incurable" diseases and lengthen the life span, it may seem that we have reason to put "faith" in the technologies and their specialists. But illness and death restore our perspective on how limited technology is and remind us who really is in charge. Humility is a realistic and comforting response to our being mortal creatures, especially when shared in a community of humble people. When we have reached the limits of what we have and what we can do, humility speaks the truth: God is still there, on our side, passionately involved with us, loving each of us without end.

◆ Patience is the virtue closely allied to perseverance and humility. Yet patience is not a typical characteristic of patients or of those who care for them. The problems of growing old, sickness, protracted pain, debilitation, curtailed movement, and the inability to obtain relief create situations that provoke anger, frustration, and bitterness. Patience demands taking control of ourselves when panic threatens to hurl us in all directions. Patience gets trivialized as a virtue when it is interpreted as pure passivity. Patience as purposeful waiting is based on the firm conviction that good will be victorious eventually, that suffering need not be futile, and that God will prevail in the end.

But to be patient is not easy, especially in a culture that prizes immediate results and that accepts depression, despair, and sometimes even taking one's life as appropriate responses when things do not quickly turn in one's favor. Patience steers us on a different course. In the spirit of Jesus who bore affliction patiently, we learn that patience invites us to remain courageous and confident in the hope that God cares, is at work righting the wrongs and healing all hurts, and will ultimately triumph.

◆ Hope, also allied to patience, is the virtue tinged with defiance. It refuses to live by the judgment that the future is closed and that we have nowhere to go. Hope imagines what is possible, even in the face of limitation and death. Hope is rooted in the fundamental biblical truth that all possibilities for life and its future stem from the goodness of God. Hope is confident that life is more reliable than unreliable and that the basis of all things is the fundamental graciousness of God's love which is constant and undefeatable. This is most clearly evident in Jesus being raised from the dead. The resurrection of Jesus (the best of all possible futures) is our ultimate guarantee of hope.

Hope is the virtue that banks on the promises of Jesus Christ. One promise concerns the present: whatever we have now on earth is not complete because it will be transformed by God. Another concerns the victory over suffering and death: Jesus conquered death and thereby gave us eternal life. Hope is a resilient virtue that enables the healing community to carry on its mission of proclaiming the nonfinality of death and the transformation of suffering.

> Illness and death restore our perspective on how limited technology is and remind us who really is in charge.

A community of care might inspire hope by providing a framework of spirituality that gives meaning and hope to the aging so that suffering and decline have purpose in life. Unlike our culture which supports the notion that human fulfillment is the product of relentless activity in the world, our spiritual tradition values letting go of earthly life and preparing the self for eternal life. Also, one of the foundations of the Catholic spiritual tradition is that suffering, when accepted for loving reasons, has redemptive meaning. Without that spiritual commitment, "better living through chemistry" becomes more than a chemical company's slogan; we risk encouraging merely technical ("curing") solutions to the inevitabilities of being mortal creatures, and we may lose sight of human wholeness as the goal of care not only in the middle of life but also at its final edge.

A Community of Hospitality

Becoming a community of interdependence and care is activated by hospitality, offering people the warmth of a welcoming response when they are away from their homes. The Second

Vatican Council highlighted this quality by describing the Church, and life itself, as a pilgrimage. In this sense, every person requires hospitality, for we are all pilgrims, passing through this world on the way to eternal life. All the more, then, do the dying need hospitality.

One of the ways this hospitality is being provided today is through hospice care. "Hospice" originally meant a lodging for travelers. Today, instead of being a particular place, hospice is a concept of care which should pervade the whole healthcare delivery system and thereby restore the art of relationships to healthcare. We have already met "hospice" in Part III as an institutional response for relieving pain in the clinical setting. We learned that the purpose of hospice care is to create an environment in which one maintains the best quality of life possible while dying peacefully, without actively prolonging life or hastening death.

Three characteristics of hospice satisfy many of the requirements for the virtue of hospitality. It respects the multiple dimensions of the patient's total good; it improves the conditions of dying; and it reaches beyond the patient to the patient's network of support.

Repect for the Patient's Total Good

First, hospitality improves the quality of mercy we extend by attending to the patient's total good. The patient's physical well-being is certainly at center stage in healthcare, but physical good is merely one part of the patient's total good. The depth and complexity of the patient's good includes more than the positive physical effects medical interventions can bring. The healthcare profession's commitment to healing requires attention to the entire person. Thus, we cannot look at major health issues in purely medical terms. We must respect the reciprocal relation of the physical and spiritual dimensions of the patient as an "embodied spirit," or "inspirited body."

If healing is to address the whole person, then pastoral care is as essential to treatment as are the interventions provided by other healthcare professionals. Pastoral care in a community of hospitality is not something administered as an afterthought, or consolation prize, when the healthcare specialists can do no more. It must be an integral part of the plan of treatment and be delivered with the same competence we expect from all healthcare professionals.

The challenge of this integrated view of the patient as a person is to treat the dying person not only as a patient with physical symptoms but also as a person needing love and seeking a sense of significance. The hospitable community of faith can share stories and insights from the Christian tradition to assure the dying that their lives are not meaningless and that they are not suffering alone. Pastoral caregivers especially can be the companions who enable the dying to reach into their own experiences of life and into their tradition of faith to find comfort and meaning.

Often, telling the story of their life becomes a way for the dying to acknowledge that their time in this world has made a difference. By describing what they accomplished in life and by naming what they found meaningful or fulfilling as well as what made them (and others) happy, the dying are able to discover how they want to be remembered. They are able to see concretely that their love has not been lost in the lives of those they touched.

The pastoral caregiver can suggest ways to interpret these memories by sharing images of faith. Reflecting upon the Scriptures, for example, can enable patients to see how their lives reenact God's saving history and what contribution they have made to God's purposes. In the same way, a pastoral caregiver can help patients connect their suffering to that of Jesus and become witnessés of the transforming power of God in their lives. This type of connection may not relieve all the anxiety a dying person feels, but it does bring the person closer to the mystery of death and the realization that "Christ is still pained and tormented in his members, made like him" (Rite, no. 2).

Improvement of the Conditions of Dying

The second characteristic of the hospitable community is that it improves the conditions of dying. Hospice care focuses on comfort rather than cure. The importance of controlling symptoms includes managing pain, nausea, vomiting, and other reactions as effectively as possible. Preventing pain before it begins rather than administering pain relief as needed, for example, would be one of the main features which sets a community of hospitality apart from any other hospital community. In light of the available medicines and methods to control pain, no dying patient needs unwillingly to bear great pain today. In a community of hospitality, the dying ought to be able to live as free from pain and as much in control as possible.

> Hospice is a concept of care which should pervade the whole healthcare delivery system and thereby restore the art of relationships to healthcare.

The clinical discussion in Part III showed us that pain is more than just physical. So, our approach to the psycho-social-spiritual pain must be addressed in multidisciplinary ways and incorporated in a comprehensive ministry of care. These dimensions of pain cannot be reached by medications but only by the compassionate presence of members of the caring community.

We have learned that one dimension of pain is loneliness. While an autopsy may report the clinical event of a heart attack, the actual cause of death may really be the "broken heart" of loneliness. Suffering, as life ends, is exacerbated for some if they are unable to form and to sustain relationships of meaning and value. Caregivers can support these relationships while a community of faith can amplify them through its symbols, stories, and rituals. To mean something to someone else or to know that you are deeply cared for is reason itself for well-being. When we find ourselves in communion with others, and when that communion is supported and nurtured, suffering is shared and thereby diminished. Yet too often the dying person's fear of isolation is only reinforced when empty gestures or casual statements of reassurance are given. Everyone who has any contact with the dying needs to be more conspicuously visible and keep company with them more often, talking about what is important to them and listening to their needs, fears, questions, and hopes. This cannot be left as a responsibility for healthcare professionals alone.

Spiritual and religious support systems are extremely important to people facing death. In the Catholic tradition, the most powerful resources are prayer and ritual, especially the thoughtful celebration of the sacraments. Prayer makes explicit and personal the community's relationship to the dying person. It brings to consciousness God's presence and allows the patient to express anguish and fear as well as his or her hope and love.

The Catholic tradition has long affirmed that sacraments are of great importance in the life of faith; they are moments which manifest the presence of a loving God in our midst and are a privileged means of heightening our experience with God's love. The Eucharist is at the heart of the Church's life as a profound encounter with the Risen Lord. The Sacrament of Reconciliation, which restores harmony with self, others, the environment, and God, can help the patient in many ways: (1) to repair broken relationships, (2) to heal the soul, (3) to integrate the person back into the community of faith, and (4) to provide a sense of forgiveness often needed to be able to face the crisis of dying. The Anointing of the Sick reflects God's compassion to strengthen the body and the soul so that the sick will not lose faith or hope but be at peace with God, others, and themselves especially during their illness.

The responsibility of hospitable care does not fall exclusively on the shoulders of pastoral caregivers. Everyone who is involved with the sick and dying shares this responsibility. The Rite for the Pastoral Care of the Sick reaffirms this principle by stating: "This ministry is the common responsibility of all Christians, who should visit the sick, remember them in prayer, and celebrate the sacraments with them. The family and friends of the sick, doctors and others who care for them, and priests with pastoral responsibilities have a particular share in this ministry of comfort"

(Introduction, no. 43). This will demand giving up a little of that precious commodity of medical care — time. Hospitality does not ask for a lot of time, but it does require enough so that the weak and the dying might feel accepted and know that they enjoy a respectful place in our lives.

> Suffering, as life ends, is exacerbated for some if they are unable to form and to sustain relationships of meaning and value.

The Patient's Network of Support

The third characteristic of the hospitable community is that it reaches beyond the patient to include the patient's network of support, his or her family and caregivers. The heart of the issue in responding to chronic, debilitating, and lingering illnesses is the human heart itself. How much help does it need? The lack of support for those who have to spend endless hours caring for the terminally ill is another factor that makes euthanasia an attractive way to bring relief not only to the dying but even to those who have to care for the dying.

The responsibility to be hospitable to caregivers means health-care communities should provide: (1) sufficient relief from physically attending to the dying; and (2) structures for emotional support for those who must deal with their own fear of death, as well as the death of those to whom they have given so much time and attention.

Being hospitable to families would include: (1) providing relief help so that they can go about their business of dealing with other affairs of life; (2) providing good advice on how to get access to services which provide financial support; and (3) providing temporary housing, if that is necessary, so that families can stay together and be mutually responsible for each other's well-being while remaining close to the one who is dying.

Hospitality also includes helping the survivors to finish and to celebrate the story of their loved one by telling those parts of the story which the dying person could not or did not have time to tell. Hospitality also means listening compassionately to the shock, anger, mistrust, and hatred which survivors still feel lest it overwhelm them and lead to depression and despair. Support groups for those who are trying to cope with the death of a loved one can be very helpful, too, because they provide a comfortable place to clarify stories and to reconcile and heal what still needs to be mended.

As each person's story and circumstances are different, so too are the skills necessary to facilitate that person's experience of suffering and dying. Any one pastoral caregiver cannot be expected to be all things to all patients. This is the time when the gifts of a caring community are most needed. Some are gifted in crisis intervention, others in long-term interventions; some are gifted in prayer and ritual, while others are gifted in facilitating storytelling and interpretation. When each member contributes according to his or her particular talents, then the multidimensional needs of the patient and the patient's family are met. Adequate response to the dying will mean that the Church must be linked closely with the dying patient and the healthcare institution. The pastoral care services may be the important link in this network of interdependence that upholds basic values and sustains the communication necessary for everyone to work as partners along this final phase of life's journey.

Conclusion

By being a virtuous community of interdependence, care, and hospitality, the Catholic community gives witness to the convictions which lie behind the arguments we use to oppose euthanasia — that God is the absolute sovereign over life and death, that suffering can be transformed into eternal life, and that a healthcare system dedicated to caring and managing pain effectively would not abandon anyone to the experience of physical agony in dying. Moreover, by such virtuous living we may enhance the patient's sense of worth, meaning, and belonging while alleviating some of the fears of the sick, the elderly, or the dying. In this way, the Catholic community may be able to address many of the concerns which motivate people to consider euthanasia. By being role models of caring who offer principled rational arguments against euthanasia and assisted suicide, we can have an impact on shaping public consensus toward death as an experience we need not hasten through lethal intervention.

Implications for Catholic Healthcare

◆ Death can be something that does not just happen to us but that arises from within to bring to fulfillment all that is valuable to us. In this spirit, what practices do we have to help a patient transform the experience of dying from a mere ending of life to its personal completion?

◆ Suffering is a personal matter which has no objective measurement. What evidence is there that our caregivers make a special effort to pay attention to patients' claims of suffering and provide the medical, social, psychological, and spiritual resources which will help them to bear their suffering?

◆ Suffering and death are not absolute evils to be avoided at all costs but can be transformed by identifying with the suffering/death/resurrection of Jesus. Give examples of how we include the resources of Christian faith — its stories, symbols, and rituals — in our total care of the dying.

◆ Catholic moral principles regarding the conservation of health and life do not promote physical life as the absolute good to be prolonged "at any cost." Cite specific policies that guide us in respecting a patient's limits as to what he or she can accept as beneficial treatment in order to avoid the burdens of overtreatment or undertreatment.

◆ The moral character of our communities gives true witness to our theological and moral convictions. In what areas and by what actions do we give witness to being a virtuous community of interdependence, care, and hospitality?

◆ The ethos of individualism asserts that independence, not interdependence, is the key to human dignity. What processes are in place to lead us in examining our relationships to make sure we are committed to interdependent partnerships sustained by trust and honesty? How are we corporately attempting to be catalysts for collaboration with other communities which have an interest in the care of the dying?

◆ The paradigm of curing has dominated the delivery of healthcare so that caring is reduced to the consolation prize for a cure that could not be attained. What measures do we use in examining our overall style, plan, and goals of treatment in order to see whether the whole person is being treated and respected?

◆ Hospice care admirably embodies the virtue of hospitality. What criteria do we use to examine our present healthcare delivery methods to ensure that they respect the multiple dimensions of the patient's total good, improve the conditions of dying, and reach beyond the patient to the patient's network of support?

> By being role models of caring who offer principled rational arguments against euthanasia and assisted suicide, we can have an impact on shaping public consensus toward death as an experience we need not hasten through lethal intervention.

SUMMARY

Our goal in caring for the dying is to help them to live well until they die. To do this, we have to create an environment within our families, our culture, and our healthcare institutions in which the fear of dying does not spoil the joy of living. In short, we need to establish a hospitable place where it is literally okay and safe to die.

The goals of our efforts are reflected in the following excerpt adapted from a 1975 statement of the United Nations General Assembly.

Appropriate care of the dying means that a dying person can expect:

- To be treated as a living human being until death
- To be cared for by caring, sensitive, knowledgeable people who will attempt to understand the needs of the dying; who maintain a sense of hopefulness, however challenging that might be; and who will be able to gain some personal satisfaction in helping the dying face death
- To receive continuing medical and nursing attention, even though goals of curing must be changed to goals of only caring
- To express feelings and emotions about approaching death; to discuss and enlarge religious or spiritual experiences, or both, regardless of what they may mean to others
- To participate in decisions concerning care; and not to be judged for such decisions, which may be contrary to the beliefs of others
- To die in peace and dignity, and not alone
- To be free from pain
- To have questions answered honestly, and not to be deceived
- To have help from and for one's family in accepting death
- To expect that the sanctity of one's body will be respected after death.

ENDNOTES

1. *Cruzan v. Director, Missouri Department of Health*, 497 U.S. 261, 1990.

2. Congregation for the Doctrine of the Faith, *Declaration on Euthanasia*, U.S. Catholic Conference, Washington, DC, Publication 704-9, 1980.

3. Henry Campbell Black, *Black's Law Dictionary*, 6th edition, West Publishing Co., St. Paul, MN, 1990, p. 554.

4. Congregation for the Doctrine of the Faith.

5. Black, p. 988.

6. Black, p. 1438.

7. Black, p. 734.

8. Derek Humphry, *Final Exit: The Practicalities of Self-Deliverance and Assisted Suicide for the Dying*, The Hemlock Society, Eugene, OR, 1991.

9. National Conference of Catholic Bishops, "Guidelines for Legislation of Life-Sustaining Treatment," *Origins*, U. S. Catholic Conference, January 24, 1985, pp. 526-528.

10. National Conference of Catholic Bishops, *A Commentary on the Uniform Rights of the Terminally Ill Act*, U.S. Catholic Conference, Washington, DC, June 1986.

11. Committee for Pro-Life Activities, National Conference of Catholic Bishops, "Nutrition and Hydration: Moral and Pastoral Reflections," *Origins*, U.S. Catholic Conference, April 9, 1992, pp. 705-712.

12. *Cruzan v. Director.*

13. *In the Matter of Westchester County Medical Center, on Behalf of Mary O'Connor*, 534 NYS 2d, 1988.

14. Congregation for the Doctrine of the Faith.

15. "Gaudium et Spes," in Austin Flannery, OP, ed., *Vatican Council II, The Conciliar and Post Conciliar Documents*, Daughters of St. Paul, Boston, MA, 1988, no. 18, pp. 917-918.

16. "Gaudium et Spes," no. 18.

17. "Gaudium et Spes," no. 18.

18. Pope John Paul II, *On the Christian Meaning of Suffering*, St. Paul Editions, Daughters of St. Paul, Boston, MA, 1984, no. 26, p. 44.

19. Pope John Paul II, no. 19, p. 30.

20. Congregation for the Doctrine of the Faith.

The Catholic Health Association of the United States is the national leadership organization of more than 1,200 Catholic healthcare sponsors, systems, facilities, and related organizations and services. Founded in 1915, CHA enables its members to accomplish collectively what they could not achieve individually. The association participates in the life of the Church by advancing the healthcare ministry and by asserting leadership within the Church and the rest of society through programs of education, advocacy, and collaboration.

This document represents one more CHA service. National headquarters: 4455 Woodson Road, St. Louis, MO 63134-3797; 314-427-2500. Washington office: 1776 K Street, NW, Suite 204, Washington, DC 20006-2304; 202-296-3993.